P9-EFJ-052

ORDINARY HAZARDS

ORDINARY HAZARDS

A MEMOIR

NIKKI GRIMES

WORDSONG
AN IMPRINT OF HIGHLIGHTS
Honesdale, Pennsylvania

ACKNOWLEDGMENT

"Evening Train" (three-line excerpt on page 107) by Denise Levertov, from *Evening Train*, copyright © 1992 by Denise Levertov. Reprinted by permission of New Directions Publishing Corp.

WordSong
An Imprint of Highlights
815 Church Street
Honesdale, Pennsylvania 18431
wordsongpoetry.com
Printed in the United States of America

ISBN: 978-1-62979-881-3
Library of Congress Control Number: 2019902537

First edition
10 9 8 7 6 5 4 3 2 1

Design by Barbara Grzeslo
The text is set in Sabon.
The titles are set in Gill Sans Light and Sabon bold italic.

For my sister, Carol,
who shared part of the journey
and knows the God of Grace,
who brought us safely through

MEMOIR:

a work of imperfect memory in which you meticulously capture all that you can recall, and use informed imagination to fill in what remains.

PROLOGUE

I can't deal with crazy.
Yeah, I know that's not politically correct,
but when you're inches away from someone's
mental and emotional avalanche, trust me,
the word crazy *is what comes to mind.*
I used to have a friend who stepped
off and on the bipolar train
once too often for me to handle.
Had to cut her loose. Had to.
I'd already taken that rough ride
with my schizophrenic mother,
and that's one ticket
I will not buy again.
It's a long story, but I'm a poet.
I can cut it short.

BOOK ONE

1950–1955

"a Self to be identified
clarified
outlined, free form
so there is room to breathe"

—Mari Evans

THE NAMING

I read somewhere that names
penetrate the core of our being,
and I suppose, this is
as good a time as any to confess
my name is not the only lie
I've ever lived with, but *Nikki* is
the first invention for which
I accept full responsibility.

Nickname is the word
I plucked it from when I was six.
I immediately liked
the hard *k* of it, which sounded
firm and looked like a sturdily braced wall,
whether I wrote block letters
or loopy cursive script.
I fiddled with the spelling for years,
eventually dropping *c*
and adding another *k*
as if it were a second layer
of brick.

Toughness is what I was after,
although I couldn't have
articulated as much.
My real name huddled
behind that wall,
along with its memories.
The girl with that name wasn't
worth a lot, at least not so you'd notice,
which I suppose was why I chose
to keep my distance. I mean, if she

was worth the space she occupied,
why'd someone lock her away?
Why'd she take unearned beatings
from strangers?
Why'd her own mother—never mind.
For now, let's just say the girl with that
old name suffered things I wanted to forget.
Besides, few people managed to
pronounce my birth name as intended,
and life is too short to spend
correcting everyone I meet.

I won't be revealing that name now,
but thanks kindly for your interest.
Just call me Nikki.

CARDS ON THE TABLE

1.
Cards on the table:
I have a PhD in avoidance,
which kept me running from
the past for years.
I was particularly fond of
parroting Scarlett O'Hara:
"I'll think about it tomorrow."
But now my need
for light and truth is greater than
my fear of murky memories.
Time to grab my flashlight
and step into the tunnel.

2.
I peer into the past,
pretending bravado,
but still I shiver,
as the ghosts of yesterday
come screaming into the present
without apology,
dragging more baggage
than I recall.
We're masters
of selective memory,
aren't we? Let's face it,
we're all allergic to pain.

3.
Pain can sully your soul,
if you let it,
and rage held in reserve

will turn to sludge,
will obstruct the passageway
to your heart.
You won't even
be aware of it,
but over time,
the river of your joy
slows to a trickle.
Your laughter loses
its hardy echo.
Before you know it,
rage has you so clogged up inside,
that precious little love or joy
or laughter can squeeze through.
If you're not careful,
your heart . . . just . . . stops.
Emergency surgery is required.
If you're going to survive,
those passageways
have got to be cleared.
"Doctor? Get in here, *stat*."

BORN

I could tell you a thing or two
about Harlem Hospital,
not because I was born there,
but because severe bouts
of asthma made me
an emergency-room regular.
The muscles in my mother's arms
must have burned from the ache
of carrying me there
night after night,
which I'm fairly certain
she resented.
What's important
about this detail of my birth?
Place, I suppose.
Harlem is *in* me,
which is odd in a way.
One of the few pictures I have
of my ebony self back then
shows skinny me
peering out at the world
through heavy bifocals,
standing on the streets of Harlem,
looking lost.

HOME

The first home that
comes to mind
had a hall running
the length of it,
rooms flagging off
from either side like
train compartments.
Eat-in kitchen,
living room, bathroom,
bedrooms in the back.
They called it a railroad flat,
perfect preparation
for the hours I would
soon spend riding
the rails.

WILDLIFE

Home was never a safe place,
as my sister, Carol, tells it.
Forget the Wild West
of inner-city streets,
bullets buzzing by
on the occasional Friday night,
propelled by a deadly combo
of alcohol and apathy.
I'm talking about *inside*,
any day of the week.
Sis paints the picture:
I'd be tucked into
a dresser drawer,
higher off the floor
than my crib, supposedly
out of reach of the rats
that roamed the rooms
after dark.
I can't quite remember
the hardness of the dresser drawer,
only the softness of my blanket.
I don't recall coming
nose-to-nose with any rat,
but there were mornings
I did see
an empty plastic bag
on the kitchen table
where a loaf of bread
used to be,
and the trail of breadcrumbs
across the linoleum,
a broken line
of evidence.

WITNESSES

I've cracked the past
like a door.
Things long forgotten
keep slipping through,
like the angels who
appeared at night to visit me
when I was two or three,
bright lights sent
as silent proof
that God
was always
near.

SIZE DOESN'T MATTER

Four-foot-nine.
Such a tiny person
to have her initials
carved so deeply into
the meat of my soul.
No matter how you spell it,
the word *Mother*
is too small
to suffice.

MOMMY

She was quite the beauty,
all brown doe-eyes
the size of quarters,
dimples deep enough
to dive in,
and a thick mass of
shining black curls
on which her veil rested
like a crown.
Her wedding photo with my father
smiled sweetly from
the photographer's studio window
for years,
silently selling the world
one tantalizing tale:
You, too, can enjoy
a moment of bliss
like this.

IMAGINARY FRIENDS

Mommy had a secret life,
a kind of play that was
more serious than I knew.
Sometimes I'd catch her
talking to people
who weren't there.
Finger to her lips,
she'd shush me
whenever I asked,
"Mommy, who are you
talking to?"
It would be years before
paranoid schizophrenia
grew roots
in the soil of my own
vocabulary.

WAR

Daddy was a ghost
in those early years,
moving in and out of our lives,
barely visible, like smoke.
Yelling punctuated the air
when he was there.
Mom's sharp tongue
made his ears bleed
every time he'd
gamble away
the rent money.
He nursed complaints
of his own,
like Mom draping
wet diapers
on his music stand,
a sniper attack on a man
who composed
chamber music
and played
the violin.
Cease-fires
never lasted long.

DROWNING

I wasn't the only one
in need of angels.
Dad's absences
multiplied a sadness
Mom was incapable of hiding,
though she tried by
diving into countless
glasses of something
clear as water,
with a smell that
wrinkled the nose.
I sipped it once
when she wasn't looking,
and spat it out,
the bitter taste chasing
my tongue from the comfort
of my mouth.
Why would she coat her throat
with something that could only
strip her taste buds bare?

NIGHTMARE

Dad gone for good,
we moved in with Mom's cousin
and her grown boys, for a while.
In the bedroom across the hall,
the boys often entertained themselves
with needles of joy juice.
That's what they called it
between bouts of laughter,
heads lolling back, eyes the color
of a blood moon.
Sometimes, they'd moan
and Carol would rock me on her lap
while Mom prayed over us
pleading for protection.

One day, Mom decided
prayer was not enough.
She confronted—
let's call her Sadie—
to lodge a complaint
about her boys shooting heroin
right where we could see.
A fight broke out between them,

and Sadie cracked Mom in the head
with an iron.
Blood gushed everywhere,
to the tune of me screaming.
But it was all delirium, wasn't it?
Some bad dream born of
indigestion? That had to be it.
I was certain right up until

the night, years later,
when Mom took my index finger
and placed it on her scar.
"The next day," she said,
"we moved away."

ON OUR OWN

1.
No one warned me
the world was full of
ordinary hazards
like closets with locks and keys.

I learned this lesson when Mom,
without her cousin to fall back on,
left us daily with
a succession of strangers
while she went to work.
One woman was indisputably
a demon in disguise,
full lips grinning slyly
as Mom waved goodbye
each morning.
"See you after work,"
Mom said that first day.
The second she was out of sight,
Demon's smile melted like
hot paraffin.
Snatching up Carol and me,
she dragged us, kicking, to
the bedroom closet.
She shoved us in, quick as the witch
in "Hansel and Gretel,"
jamming the key in the lock.
"You tattle to your mom about this,"
she growled, "I'll come back
and beat the black off ya."
Deadly threat delivered,
she left for the day.

2.
I screamed, my puny fists pounding the door
till Carol caught me by the wrists
and held me still. "Shhhh," she whispered.
"It's okay. I'm right here."
Once my breathing slowed,
Carol left me long enough
to navigate the darkness.

She found suitcases to sit on.
Sniffling, I perched on the edge of one
and pressed my fingertips together.

"Now I lay me down to sleep,
I pray the Lord my soul to keep."

I repeated those words
like a chant.
I was three years old.
It was the only prayer I knew.

3.
I should've prayed not to pee my pants.
The cramped and stuffy space
made me wheeze.
Brass fittings on the Samsonite case
dug into the flesh
behind my knees.
But worse yet,
the occasional roach
skittered along my calf,
up a thigh,
and I would scratch
and stomp and cry
till it was off.

No one was around
to wipe away my tears,
except my sister,
who had tears of her own.

4.
Day after day,
the routine remained unchanged.
Demon locked us up in the morning,
then let us out and fed us just before
Mom came home from work.
Despite the witch's threat,
the minute Carol saw Mom, she poured out
the horrors of that first day,
but Mom waved her away
with a warning
to quit lying.

5.
One afternoon,
when I thought
we'd live in the dark forever,
I heard what sounded like
a familiar voice.
"Girls?"
"Mommy?" I screamed,
afraid to believe.
But the lock turned,
the door flew open,
and I leaped into Mom's arms.
"My God!" she said.
"How long have you two
been in here?"
"All day," snapped Carol,

keeping her distance.
"I told you!
I told you,
but you called me a liar!"

6.
The slap of words sent
Mom to her knees, *please*
written all over her face.
"I'm so sorry," she whispered,
reaching for my sister.
Carol backed away.
"Jesus," Mom said. "What did
this woman do? Are you all right?"
Where to begin?
There were too many answers.
Even my big sister
lacked the language needed
for them all,
so we chose silence.
Besides, it was impossible to guess
which atrocities
Mom was
prepared to hear.

7.
Thankfully, my sister and I
never laid eyes on that
bit of walking evil again. Still,
Demon lived inside us for years,
embedded in our twin fears
of the dark.

MISSING DADDY

I missed the cushion
of Daddy's soft voice,
the sleepy lullaby
of his violin
as his bow
gently kissed
each string.
Even Mom's
occasional hugs
were not as warm
an embrace.

FAMILY

Uncle Abe.
Aunt Esther.
Uncle Willis.
Aunt Lorraine.
Uncle Gene.
Aunt Edna.
On the face of it,
we had family aplenty.
One question,
never answered:
Where were they all
when Carol and I
were small?

A PROPER INTRODUCTION

Sorry.
I neglected to
paint you a picture of myself.
I began as a baby
with chunky cheeks
that invited pinching,
then, by five or six,
transformed into a tallish
brown twig of a girl,
cursed with an enormous nose
(in my rough estimation)
and a small face
swallowed up by
oversized eyeglasses,
like my sister's,
with lenses so thick
they slowed the speed of light.
I was quite sure "pretty"
was not
in my future.

BINGE

Babysitters came and went,
with Mom pulling in
all the overtime
she could manage,
taking the edge off of each day
with a shot, or two, or three
of blackberry brandy.
Sometimes, she'd disappear
in an alcoholic haze
and be missing for days,
leaving no one at home
to watch over us.
Carol, nearly five years my senior,
would play little mama,
mixing raw oats and buttermilk
for us to eat—
anything to fill our bellies.
Someone must have noticed us alone
and telephoned Child Services.

The policeman and
the freckle-faced lady
who came to our door
smiling
asked if we knew
where our mommy was,
or our daddy.
When we shook our heads *no*,
they took us away.
I tugged my big sister's hand.
"Carol? Are they taking us to jail?"

“No,” she said. So why did they
pile us in a police car,
like we were guilty
of some crime?

AFTERMATH

They kept us together
for two years,
serving us up
to strangers,
a merry-go-round of
unfamiliar places,
unknown faces of people
with names my tears
washed away.
Don't ask me
how many homes,
or where.
Those days are lost.
I held on to nothing except
my sister's hand.

JERSEY

I recall being five,
doing foster-time
at a temporary placement
across the George Washington Bridge
in Jersey:
a detached A-frame floats into view,
red brick, with the suggestion
of a lawn out front,
a place that screamed *wholesome*.
Inside, Carol and I were whipped
whenever the foster parents' progeny
misbehaved and pointed
in our direction.

Carol woke me one sunrise.
"Quiet," she warned in a whisper,
then bundled me, like a bear,
in heavy clothing
and crept down the stairs
with me tiptoeing behind.
On the hall table,
she found the lady's purse,
made a few dollars disappear
without the use of magic,
then motioned to the front door.
A few more careful steps,
and we were gone,
racing downhill in first light,
dodging patches of ice
from the last snow.
A neighbor's dog snarled as we passed,
and I stuck to the spot, trembling.

"Don't worry," Carol comforted me,
"he's on a leash." I breathed easier.
"Carol?" I asked, starting to walk again,
"Where are we going?" Not that it mattered.
I'd have followed her anywhere.

LONG DISTANCE

A forever ride of subway trains
and buses
led us to Grandma's house
in Washington Heights.
We rang her bell,
listened for the crackle
of the intercom.
Her tinny voice came through.
"Who is it?"
"Hi, Grandma," I said.
"It's me." "And me," said Carol.
"Good God!" she said.
"What are you doing here?"
Before we could answer,
she rang us in.

She shuffled to her door
in robe and pajamas,
but already wearing
her perfectly coiffed
reddish-brown wig
to hide her early-onset
female-pattern baldness.
Grandma got
right to the point.
"What are you two doing here?"
Carol explained while I
took in the living room.
The sofa was slick
with that horrible plastic cover
that stuck to your butt
when you sat on it,
especially in the heat of summer,

but it was big enough
for my sister and me
to sleep on,
and that's all that mattered.

"Why didn't you call your mother?"
Grandma asked.
Carol and I gave each other a look.
"We don't know where she is now."
"Lord," said Grandma.
"Well, you can stay here—
for a few days. But that's it.
I've already raised my kids.
I'm done."
Her words slammed me in the face
like a door.
Did we do something wrong?
Is that why no one wants us?
Troubled thoughts
clung to me like shadow
through the day,
and sleep that night
was fitful.
Still, no nightmare visited
till morning
when Children's Services
slipped in quietly
to take us away—
Carol to one home,
me to another.

As I walked out the door,
I dried my eyes
so Grandma could clearly see
my hatred.

MARCH KIDNAP

Anger and I
stood stiff on the train platform
next to Mr. Klein,
the social worker,
his thin face a pasty white oval,
nose straight as a ferret, lips pouty,
his cat-gray eyes peering from
wire-rimmed glasses,
his hair a dirty-blond cap
of spring-loaded curls.
Every now and then,
I stomped my cold feet
to keep them from getting numb.
Inches from Mr. Klein,
I gripped my suitcase with one hand
and buried the other in my pocket
so he couldn't reach out and hold it
as if he had a right.
He was taking me away from my sister,
taking me—where?
That's when the tears came,
each drop following the salty trail
already marked.

TRAIN RIDE

I kneeled on the tweed-covered seat,
bifocals pressed against the sooty window.
"Sit properly,"
Mr. Social Worker told me,
as if that mattered.
Ignoring him, I watched the sun
turn the river into a mirror,
in some places solid enough
to walk on, in others broken
into odd bits, like my family—
pieces of light scattered.

Where'd they take my sister?

More than an hour passed
before the ticket-taker
strode through the train car
belting out, "Ossining!
Next stop, Ossining!"
which is where
my future waited.

The Mystery of Memory #1

Author and storyteller,
I cry out for order,
logical sequences,
and smooth transitions.
A modicum of skill
allows me to create as much—
in story. But here?
Where is the chronology of a life
chaotic from the start?
There is no certainty of sequence,
no seamless transitions,
nothing as neat and orderly as that.
Only scraps of knowing
wedged between blank spaces,
flashes of who, what, and when
to capture as best I can—
a poor offering, I know,
but I am the widow,
and this is my mite.

BOOK TWO

1955–1960

"It is you who light my lamp; the Lord, my God lights up my darkness."

—Psalm 18:28

Search my life for luck,
and bad is all you'll find.
Keep an eye out
for grace, though.
Hard evidence appears
round every corner.
It is the invisible bridge
spanning the abyss,
the single light
that outstrips the dark
every time.

THE FAMILY BUCHANAN

Anne Sharrock Buchanan,
a five-foot-eight-inch woman,
light-skinned and sturdy,
met us at the door,
her husband, James,
a walnut-colored man
beside her.
The word *crowded*
popped into my mind.
Several children
crowded the entryway.
The narrow hallway
we stepped into
was covered with
sand-colored wallpaper,
busy with bouquets
of pink roses
that crowded every
square inch of vertical space.
A slim mahogany console,
barely wide enough to hold
daily mail and house keys,
crowded the corridor,
squeezed in
next to the radiator.
Everything about this place
seemed crowded.
How could there possibly be
room enough for me?

Too many pairs of eyes
stared in my direction.

I half-hid behind Mr. Klein,
ready to follow him
into the living room,
partly because there was
a dog barking outside
that didn't sound very friendly,
and partly because
there was no place else
for me to be,
and I wanted to get away.

"Come in! Come in
so that I can close out the cold,"
said the walnut-colored man
named Mr. Buchanan.
"March is not going out like a lamb!"
One by one,
each person was introduced—
the mom, the dad,
Grace, Michael, Kendall, Brad.
We sat around the living room,
forced and fidgeting until
Mr. Klein said his goodbyes.
Mr. Buchanan showed him to the door,
flashing a kind smile that made me shiver.
I'd been fooled by a smile before.
I bit my lip, gripped my suitcase,
and waited for instructions.
"Does she talk?" asked Kendall.
"She will when she wants to,"
said his mom.
If I want to, I thought.
"For now, just take her upstairs.
Show her to her room."
Kendall, not much bigger than me,

headed upstairs, jabbering away
to fill the spaces
my silence left behind.
All his chatter,
and I heard nothing except
a few creaks in the stairs,
and that one dog barking.

THE ROOM

The dark-paneled walls
absorbed whatever
scraps of moonlight
made it past the windowsill.
Still, the room would do.
I checked the door.
No keyhole. No lock.
No chance anyone
would seal me up in there.

LASSIE'S TWIN

The day after I arrived,
I found out the family
and that barking dog
were related.
His name was Clancy,
and he was big enough to ride.
The first morning,
as I settled on a padded chair
in the oversized kitchen,
a thoroughbred collie
squeezed through
a doggy door
I hadn't noticed before,
and skidded across
the checkered linoleum,
straight for me.
He sniffed my feet,
then licked them
until I joined him
under the breakfast table.
He flicked his rough tongue
over my glasses,
and when I reached out
to pet him,
he pushed his head
against my palm,
waiting for a rub.
That's when I knew
the two of us
would get along just fine.
The parakeet,
which spent

as much time
out of the cage as in,
was another matter
altogether.

THE HOUSE ON HILL STREET

With Clancy on my heels,
I looked around the house,
an aging, two-story
brown-shingled affair with an attic,
holding its own as the first house
on the corner of a residential street,
its property edging a building
with a faded sign that said CON EDISON.
At the top of a steep,
nearly vertical incline,
the house afforded a view
of the mighty Hudson River.
The backyard boasted a gap-toothed
white picket fence on one side
with neatly trimmed bushes
on the other,
ready to sprout green
any day now, with spring
right around the corner.
Everything about this place
said *good*, said *safe*.
But was it?

SIGN LANGUAGE

A head shake
is all you need.
Up and down for *yes*,
side to side for *no*.
Three days in,
and these people still
hadn't heard my voice.

Petition

Help me, Lord.
I don't know these people.
If Carol was here,
I'd slip into bed with her.
Do you have a lap
I can crawl up on?
Stay with me.
Please.
And tell my sister
I miss her.

ANOTHER COUNTRY

The backyard pantry
was a fascination.
Big as my room,
it was a place
where rake and pruner,
shovel and shears,
fit neatly, exactly
in their designated space,
seeming more at home
than me.

MANNERS

Early lessons in manners
came back to me.
Yes, please,
no, thank you,
excuse me,
were useful words
to slip in
through the day.
They came in handy
at the dinner table.
Who needed more
than that?

Ken was probably the one
to pry a mouthful
of words from me.
That first week,
he heard me
cry myself to sleep.
The next morning,
he asked why I was crying
and what I was afraid of.
"I wasn't crying," I lied,
"and who said I was afraid
of anything?"
Not waiting for an answer,
I brushed past him
and ran down to the kitchen,
worn out from all that
speaking.

STATISTICS

Mrs. Buchanan
took me to see
a man we'll call Dr. Stern,
a psychologist we foster kids
were assigned to.
Mrs. B. called it
a routine visit
all her new fosters
had to check off the list.
She would know
all about doctors,
being receptionist
for the only black doctor
in town.
She settled me on
a waiting-room bench.
"I'll be back," she said,
patting my shoulder before
slipping out the door
to run errands.
I swung my legs anxiously
until I heard my name.
An assistant led me
toward Dr. Stern's office,
his door cracked
as he talked to someone
on the phone.
"Yeah, the next kid's file's a mess:
mentally ill alcoholic mother,
victim of abuse,
suffered abandonment—
No telling

what dark thoughts
are swimming
in that little head.
There's no chance in hell
this kid will make it—
Oh! Listen, I have to go," he said,
then hung up.
"Hello!"
I stepped into the room,
teeth clenched
tight as my fists.
Who was this stranger to say
I wouldn't make it?
He didn't know me for spit!
I gritted my way though
his silly exams,
stoking his words like kindling,
hoping to God he'd choke
on his inkblots
and "games"
of free association,
all of which taught him zero
about who I was,
or would be.
Or could be.
I am not
who he thinks.
I am me.
I am me.
I AM ME!

DEAR CAROL

Dear Carol,
I'm writing you this fake letter
I'll never get to send.
No one will tell me where they took you.
I need somebody to talk to,
somebody who knows
the right way to say my name.
You hear anything from Mom?
Moms aren't supposed to leave
little kids home alone.
I hope the corner store
runs out of her stupid brandy.

WAITING

For Mom to call.
For Mom to collect me.
But did she?
The days
rolled themselves into
a big, fat ball,
tangling me into
weeks and months,
and all they did
was take me along
for the ride.

THE SCENT OF PURPLE

Lilacs blooming
outside my window.
Never knew purple
could smell so good.

FRAGILE

1.
Curled into a ball of flannel
and inch-thick cotton bedspread,
my spindly six-year-old body
shivered, nonetheless.
Kendall and Brad in the next room
trampolined on bunk beds,
lost in laughter.
"Quiet!" yelled Mrs. Buchanan,
pausing at my door.
"Everything all right?" she asked.
I nodded. "Well, good night."
She casually extinguished the light,
and I dove deeper under the covers.
Stepping into the hall,
she closed the door behind herself
and left me cotton-mouthed,
listening for the sound of a key
turning, turning, turning in the lock
before I remembered
there was none.
I won't cry, no matter what,
I swore, biting my lip,
waiting for something
to reach out for me,
waiting for the tears that
welled up every night
for weeks.
I'm not afraid. I'm not afraid.
I'm not afraid, I repeated,
not until I wasn't,
but until I finally
fell asleep.

2.

Each night,
the terror returned
seconds after the light
was switched off.
I closed my eyes
and rocked myself
from side to side,
pleading for entrance into
the land of Nod,
too weak to storm the gates.
Hours passed, and
sleep remained elusive.
"Enough!" I said out loud one night,
reaching for my glasses
and creeping from bed.
I inched across the floor
on tiptoe.
With one desperate swipe,
I threw the switch
and sent the demons packing.
Kendall, on his way to
the bathroom, no doubt,
must have noticed
the light under my door
because he softly knocked
and asked, "Are you all right?"
"I'm fine," I whispered
loud enough for him
to leave me alone.
I didn't have much
in the world, but
my fears
were my own.

ISOLATION STATION

The house was full, but with strangers,
and I was there by myself in the dark, in a
tiny pocket of a room with a tiny bed to sleep in
and little space for the fears I'd packed in my suitcase,
which makes no sense, because why would I bring them with me?
And the night sounds, foreign to this city girl, left me tossing and
turning. There was no more room in my head to hold the anger
rising like steam, searing the edges of my brain, there was not even
a shelf where I could stack the questions crying out for answers
that wouldn't come: *Why did Mom love liquor more than Carol,*
more than me? Why did Daddy let strangers take us away?
Why did Grandma refuse to come to our rescue?
Why didn't they love us? Why didn't anyone love us enough?
Whywhywhywhwhywhywhywhywhywhy? Why?

"Stop!"

I leaped out of bed, switched on the light,
grabbed a piece of paper and a pen,
stabbed the page, and let my thoughts gush like a geyser,
shooting high into the moonless sky,
then falling down on the page I held captive
till every line was stained with my feelings and
the heat of them finally had a chance to cool, and
suddenly, I could breathe, breathe, breathe and
there was once again room enough in my head
and my heart to just—be.
Then I closed my eyes.
And it was morning.

SECRET

I slipped the tear-smudged page
into my dresser drawer.
Those words were strictly for
God and me. Besides,
this writing thing
was some kind of magic trick
I didn't yet understand,
except for this:
Magicians rarely share
their secrets.

JOURNEY

My life in notebooks
began with this,
a poem here,
an observation there,
a rage of red ink—
each sheet of white
a paper haven.
The blank page
was the only place
I could make sense
of my life,
or keep record of
each space
I called home.
The daily march of words
parading from my pen
kept me moving
forward.

Notebook

Mrs. B. put a night-light in my room.
Somebody must have told her I'm afraid of the dark.

Don't tell me lilacs aren't just the most perfect flower, ever.
I put some in a jelly jar, set them on the table in front of Mrs. B.,
and—poof—her smile came out of hiding.

Lilacs smell
like joy
moving in
for a visit.

BAPTIST BEGINNINGS

One Sunday,
the family took me to
Star of Bethlehem
for the first time.
I slid into the pew,
closed my eyes,
and listened to the organ,
letting the music hug me
on the inside.

Notebook

"Don't get comfortable,"
my foster sister Grace tells me.
"You don't belong here."
Thanks a lot! Like I don't know
I don't belong anywhere . . .

Notebook

I was supposed to go see Mom this weekend, but my visit got canceled. My social worker called and told Mrs. B. and me that Mom had a nervous breakdown, which made no sense. "How can nerves break?" I asked Mrs. B. once she hung up the phone. She told me there was nothing wrong with Mom's nerves, that she was another kind of sick, in her mind. "Right now, your mom doesn't know what's real, and what isn't."

The minute she said it, I shivered. I remembered the times I'd seen Mom talking to imaginary friends. "You mean like talking to someone who isn't there?" I asked Mrs. B. "Exactly," she said. She asked how I knew, and I just shrugged.

Mrs. B. told me I could visit Mom another time, once she felt better. Now that I know what kind of sick she is, I'm really not in any hurry.

CHANGE OF SEASON

Spring spun into summer,
the sun beat the ground
like a drum, bees hummed,
and flowers flaunted their colors.
Then my mother called,
the one who still
didn't seem to want me back,
and I was suddenly chilly again
from my head
to my heart.

Notebook

Mrs. B. is allergic to silly. She must be.
I never hear her laugh . . .

I sing around the house all the time. Ken says
I should join the choir.
God, what do you think?
Me too.
Most people only want to talk to you once a week. But
you know me, God. I could live at church.

Pssst!
Come close,
and I'll tell you
God's secret:
Music is
His most favorite thing.
There are bands in the Bible,
strumming harps,
blowing trumpets,
thumping tambourines
and cymbals, too.
"Play something!" say the angels.
But I don't know how.
"Sing, then!" say the angels.
So, I do.

FIRST LOVE

Hill Street was a sweet-smelling,
rainbow-tinted place in summer,
thanks to the trellis of
American Beauty roses
that hugged the house,
a tangle of wild grapevines,
a patch of violets and anemones,
and the saucer-sized
white hydrangeas
and blue hydrangeas
that challenged the bushes
for attention.
A carpet of lemongrass and clover
begged me to lie down,
and every day it didn't rain,
I obliged.

Notebook

Mr. B. gives me daddy hugs whenever he sees I need one.
I've got one more reason to like him:
We have music in common.
I often hear his sweet baritone
humming around the house, just because.

Brad is like my little mascot, following me everywhere.
He gets away with it 'cause he's so cute . . .

Kendall's younger than me,
but he's like my big brother,
always making sure I'm okay.

Michael ignores me. Just as well.
Ask me, trouble is his shadow.
If he's not careful, he'll end up
down the road in Sing Sing.
Funny name for a prison.

FIRST LIGHT

One July night
too sticky for bedclothes,
Ken and I camped in the yard,
counting stars you can't see
in the city.
"Be right back," he said,
returning later
with proof that
the North Star
had earthly competition.
"Here," he said,
proudly bestowing on me
a magical jar
housing temporary tenants:
my first fireflies,
dancing on air!

Notebook

My first solo, "This Little Light of Mine."
I tried fixing my hair to make it special, but couldn't get it right.
Grace rolled her eyes when I asked for help, but she did it anyway.
Guess she doesn't hate me, after all . . .

Michael was out all night. Drinking and doing drugs, according to Grace. She said Mrs. B. doesn't play that.
By this afternoon, Michael was gone . . .

Dance class! Mrs. B. says I get to take ballet.
My favorite part so far? The slippers.

Met Lori today. She lives down the street.
Says she wants to be my friend.
Didn't know how much I was missing one until then . . .

GRAPE ESCAPADE

My assignment clear:
pick grapes from the vine for jam.
No more, no less—right?
I confess, the grape taste-test
was strictly my own idea.

NO PICNIC

The park at the foot of Hill Street
provided all the space needed
for a family Labor Day cookout.
Ken and Brad's cousins arrived,
with aunts, uncles,
and a grandmother thrown in
who gave me a once-over.
The fried chicken
and corn on the cob were tasty,
but meeting some of those
extra relatives
was about as sweet
as sauerkraut.
"You must be the new one,"
said an aunt,
comparing me to who?
"You know James and Anne," said another,
"always taking in strays, God bless 'em."
Kendall, busy making his hot dog disappear,
missed the comment, but noticed
me suddenly drop my eyes.
He came running too late
to keep the cut
from stinging.
A few words—just enough
to remind this outsider
who she didn't belong to.
For me,
this beautiful family
was only
borrowed.

Notebook

I caught a fish—imagine! Catfish. Ugliest thing I've ever seen,
but I caught it. Mr. B. taught me how. Mrs. B. cleaned it. Yuck!
What a mess.
When she fried it up, I took a taste.
Sorry, Fish. You were good.

We made ice cream! I didn't know you could do that.
I got to crank the machine. Somebody should have told me
how much hard work it would be just to make a little bit
of vanilla goodness. It took forever waiting for the ice cubes
to crack and melt, for the vanilla, cream, and sugar mixed in
to get all thick and creamy. Man, I thought my arm would fall off.
It was worth it, though. Yum!
I shared it with Lori, then we rode our bikes around the
neighborhood till it was time to go in for the night.

Summer's over, and I started school. It's called Claremont,
and I think I'm going to like it. Some of the kids on my block
go there, too. At least there'll be a few familiar faces.

OCTOBER SURPRISE

Birthday celebrations
in foster care
are rare.
Who bothers about
the day you were born?
But when I turned seven,
Mrs. B. baked
a chocolate cake
with buttercream icing.
I don't recall
anyone baking me
a birthday cake before.
Maybe that's why
I baptized my first slice
with tears.

Notebook

This birthday was almost perfect. A card from Mom was waiting for me in my room, and a box from Daddy. If only Carol was here to help me open it.

PLAYGROUND

Occasional rain showers
kept me from the playground.
"You will not be coming in here
with an asthma attack
or pneumonia!"
said Mrs. B.
In good weather, though,
I raced to the park
and staked my claim daily.
The swift play
of sailing down the sliding board
was always quick fun.
Hard pumping the swing
high enough to scratch the sun
was a dream.
But the seesaw was the best,
me straddling one end,
Lori perched on the other,
both ready to test
how perfectly two friends
could push off the ground,
then spread our arms like eagles
skimming the air,
balanced there,
owning the moment,
sharing forever
in a smile.

ONE YEAR GONE

God deals days
like a deck of cards,
shuffling and counting out
kings, hearts, jokers
fast as lightning.
His hand is quicker
than my eye.

Notebook

How do blind people cross the street?
I honestly wanted to know, but just try getting an adult
to answer a question!
Since they were too busy today, I just closed my eyes
and stepped off the curb. Simple, right?
Mrs. B. sent me to the backyard for a switch.
My legs still sting. No more crossing the street
with my eyes closed.

Guess what, Sis? I'm in first grade, now.
I kind of like it. My friend, Lori, goes there, too.

My teacher taught us this French song.
"Alouette," and we got to make a famous tower
out of pipe-cleaners. It's called Eye-something,
and it's in Paris. Where's Paris?
Where are you?

WORD PLAY

Maybe it was my father's
unlucky affection
for games of chance
that made me look askance
at losing.
Or maybe Sore Loser
was my middle name
from birth.
Either way,
words plucked randomly
from Webster's
provided my preferred
mode of play
like the word *dictionary*:
dirt, *diction*, *dairy*, *drain*,
rain, *train*, *ration*,
road, *toad*,
yard.
Ditch Monopoly,
checkers, cards.
My game had no special name,
but I could play all day
and always come out
the winner.

Notebook

Mom's all better now. She left the hospital months ago. She called, asking me to come and visit for the weekend. Half of me wants to. The other half isn't so sure. The social worker says I'm lucky, that most kids like me have mothers who send them away and never look back. I guess he's right, but I'm just starting to fit in here. When I get back, will I feel like a stranger again, starting over?

TRAIN TRIP

It was 1957, and the biggest worry
my guardians had was whether
I'd get off at the right station.
One word whispered to the conductor
was the easy solution.
Saying yes when
the social worker suggested
I travel to the city solo
was easy.
Lori said I was brave
to travel by myself,
but *Pippi Longstocking*
came along for the ride.

I loved the way the Hudson
churned the sun's reflection
into ripples of light
as, nose pressed against the window,
I watched the landscape change.
The train squealed into
Grand Central Station soon enough,
and I disembarked,
keeping an eye out for Mom, who was
nowhere on the platform.
Impatient—an early trait—I dragged
my suitcase to the terminal on my own.

I set my patent-leather T-straps
inside the main terminal hall, and stalled.
A living, breathing whirligig of
dark-suited commuters
swirled around me,

newspapers pinned beneath their arms,
briefcases dangling at their sides.
As they hopped on and off of escalators
and sped toward the nearest exits,
I spun in their midst
desperate for a glimpse of my mother.
I'd have asked for help, but
everyone seemed in such a hurry.

"Mommy," I whispered,
"where are you?"
Fear shrunk my bronchial tubes
to nothing,
and I started wheezing.
Squeezing my eyes tight,
I fought for breath.
Don't cry. Don't cry.
Don't cry, I told myself,
gripping the handle of my suitcase
because it was something solid
to hold on to.

"You look lost." The kindly voice
belonged to a tall brown-skinned man
who suddenly towered over me.
"Can I help you?" he asked. My internal
don't-talk-to-strangers warning device
did not deploy, but then again,
my world was full of strangers.
Still, I was wary. "I'm not lost,"
I told him.
"I know exactly where I am."
He smiled and asked
if I was meeting anyone.
I nodded. "Your mother?"

Another nod.
"Mind if I wait with you?"
I shrugged. Stranger or no,
I welcomed the company.
His name was Mr. Clarke,
"Clarke with an *e*,"
he told me, then chatted on
to fill the silence.
"I know," he said, finally out of steam.
"Let's get you some ice cream.
Then I'll look for your mother."
He took me by the hand,
picked up my overnight bag
(only because I let him),
and steered me through that cavern
of marble, polished wood, and brass,
past a barbershop, newspaper vendor,
and shoeshine stand.
We stopped at a small café
inside the station
with ice cream on the menu.
He ordered two scoops,
got me seated,
said, "Wait right here,"
then disappeared.

I stared down at the double mound
of plain vanilla, thinking,
By the time I finish this,
Mom will be here.
To make certain of it,
I scooped up only half a teaspoon at a time,
and licked the sweet cream like
a sloth moving in slow motion.
One teaspoon left,
and still no Mom.

Angry, I scraped the bottom of the dish.
What if she doesn't come?
What am I supposed to do, then?
Where am I supposed to go?
That's when Mr. Clarke returned,
grinning, with my mom in tow.
She later told me how I'd cried,
but I only remember
assuring her that I was fine,
that Mr. Clarke had been kind.
He told Mom he had children of his own
and was happy to help.
Stranger or no, I'm glad I let him.
Traveling solo turned out to be
trickier than I'd thought.

HOME

Yesterday,
it was Manhattan.
Today,
it's Ossining.
In two weeks,
it will be Brooklyn.
Home may be
a four-letter word,
but it's getting
harder and harder
to spell.

Notebook

I get to take the train to the city again tomorrow.
This time to see Daddy. Feels like it's been forever.

Maybe I don't need legs.
Maybe I'd do better with wheels.
That way, I could roll myself to the city
any time my parents
decide to call.

PIZZA

On my visits,
Daddy always took me out
for pizza.
Once, over dinner,
I asked him the question
I'd been thinking about forever.
"Daddy, why didn't you
come for Carol and me?
Why did you let
the foster-care people
take us away?"
He dropped his eyes,
turned his face from me.
"I didn't know how
to take care of little girls.
I thought you'd be better off
with a family who did."
I wasn't sure
what kind of answer that was,
but I couldn't help thinking
maybe Carol and me
should've been little boys.

NINE-TO-FIVE

My father was a magician.
He would slide his bow across
the slender waist of his violin
with such a sweet caress,
both strings and hearts
would tremble.
From scroll to chin rest,
that brown body
belonged to him,
and the two of them
were glorious together.
But playing violin solos
and composing
original concertos
never paid his rent.
For that, Daddy depended on
a nine-to-five, working as a buyer
for a clothing factory.
Less than romantic,
the job did benefit me.
When I'd visit him
in the city, he'd turn
any morning of the week into
Take-Your-Daughter-to-Work Day
and help me choose
playclothes and dresses
off the rack
to take back to Ossining.
And did I mention,
his taste was impeccable?
Which explains where

my good taste originates,
whether we're talking
fashionable attire
or symphonic music.
Take your pick.

FUNNY

Funny how
on the train
back to Ossining,
I find myself thinking
I'll be glad
to get home.

Notebook

I lay in the backyard today, munching grapes from our tiny vine.
Hope Carol ended up somewhere fine as this.

Daddy was supposed to call this week, but he didn't.
I don't think he knows what promise *means.*

WORD GARDEN

Sunday afternoons,
Ken and Brad played
tug-of-war
with the funnies,
Mr. B. disappeared
behind the sports page,
and Mrs. B. absconded
with the entertainment section.
Grace had no use for the news,
which meant I had no competition
for the Sunday word scrambles
and puzzles.
A garden of words,
just for me.
Score!
If you asked me then,
that's what Sunday papers
were for.

Notebook

Lori's mom said we can't be friends anymore.
Through the screen door, I hear her dad call me Nigger.
He spits the word out, so I know it's ugly. Why doesn't Lori say anything?

Notebook

Farewell-to-Fall dance recital. I have a special part.
At first I don't know it's because the teacher doesn't want
a black body messing up her white line of ballerinas.
Once I do, I try to hide the hurt
behind a smile, and dance.

CAMOUFLAGE

Winter was welcome.
When I shivered from heartbreak,
I could blame the cold.

HOUSEBOUND

Sleep can be
a kind of magic.
Sometimes we wake
and the world's gone white,
streets and driveways
made to disappear
by an alchemy of snow
children know
exactly what to do with.
Screen doors jammed shut
by three feet of sparkly white,
Mrs. B. summoned the troops.
Winter workers
assigned to snow removal,
Ken, Brad, and I
climbed out a window
prissy Grace had no intentions
of squeezing through.
While Mrs. B. waited
for a shoveled porch
and cleared pathway,
we three attended to
the serious business
of building the season's
first fort.
What better way
to celebrate
my first snow day?
One snowball fight later,
opposite a neighbor's boys,
and Mrs. B's lid
threatened to blow.

"Get that snow shoveled
in the next five minutes,
or none of you
will be able to sit
till summer!"
"Yes, ma'am," we chimed,
stifling giggles.
Meanwhile,
I'm dancing inside,
grinning at Ken, at Brad—
my first two
true partners in crime
since Carol.

Notebook

Finally! Mom takes me to see my sister.
She lives in a place called Dobbs Ferry,
with a bunch of other kids. I can't count how many houses
they have there. We've both grown so much since
we saw each other, we spend most of the time just . . . staring.

Carol looked happy to see me, but not happy herself.
She doesn't much like where she's living,
but said it's not so bad.
I wish she could live with me.
I bet she'd love Mr. and Mrs. B.

ROUGH RIDE

Grace's old bicycle
wanted to return
to its original owner.
I showed off my
no-hands skill
one time too many,
but who could resist
the temptation?
People would pay
good money
for the steep hill
we owned.
Pedaling Hill Street
was all flight,
zero control—
a total blast
until I pumped the brakes
a little too late,
skidded sideways,
and slammed into
the wrought iron fence
protecting the park
from dangers like me.
One good crash,
and I suffered a gash
guaranteed to leave
a glorious scar.
Kendall said
careening into
that fence
was the perk
that came along

with the adventure.
(He'd done as much
a time or two.)
I hobbled up the hill bloody,
asthma inhaler
hanging from my hand.
Mrs. B. took one look
and sent me
to the medicine cabinet
without a lecture.
I knew enough
not to tell her
I was more than ready
to do it all again.

ALBUM

The family photo album
used to scream at me,
"Outsider!"
But one day, as I flipped
through the pages,
along with Kendall, Brad, and Grace,
I saw Michael and other foster kids
gone before I got there.
Then I spotted
a new photo of
Mr. and Mrs. B.,
and me:
in my pretty new hat,
alongside Ken and Brad,
smiling.

THE CALL

I finally settle in.
Guard down, I get cozy
in my new reality.
Before I know it,
I'm nine and a half,
letting the years roll by
without counting down
the days, the weeks,
the months.
And that's precisely
when it comes,
the phone call
I'd quit waiting for.
Mom had remarried,
made a new home with a place
especially for me.
Leaving the Buchanans felt
impossible
but I had to go.
How could I say no?
One mother is all you get,
and I wasn't ready
to give up on her yet.

CITY-BOUND

Genies must think
wishes are wasted
on kids like me.
Otherwise Mom would've waited
till school let out
before whisking me away
from Ossining.

When she ended that call, she said,
"If I had my way,
you'd return tonight,"
That's a good thing, right?

GOODBYE

Mom B. gave me a copy of
Little Women to take on
my new adventure.
I folded my clothing,
stacked notebooks packed
with memories,
and jammed everything
into a suitcase
I suddenly hated.
Goodbye is a word
I wouldn't even whisper.
Instead, I gave lots of hugs
and kept repeating,
"I love you, I love you,
I love you," because
somehow I knew
they deserved a gift
for tending me
in the garden of their family,
and my breaking heart
was all I had to offer.

BOOK THREE

1960–1963

"A girl with braids
sits in this corner seat, invisible,
pleased with her solitude. . . ."

—Denise Levertov
"Evening Train"

God's light everywhere,
tucked between the shadows.

The *Mystery of Memory* #2

Trauma is a memory hog.
It gobbles up all available space
in the brain,
leaves little room to mark
daily happenstances,
or even routine injuries
which are less than
life-threatening.
Innocuous classroom feuds?
Gone.
Who pulled whose hair
during fire drills?
Couldn't tell you.
The name of the new teacher
in the new school,
the mascot and location of which
were singularly unremarkable?
Don't even ask.
The bloody parade of painful days
have ground such sweet details
into a fine layer of dark dust,
blown away by time,
leaving me
with a multiplicity
of blank spots.
But don't worry.
I've bridged the gaps
with suspension cables
forged of steely gratitude
for having survived my past
at all.

LAST STOP

I was already posted near the exit
when the Hudson Line
rolled into Grand Central.
I looked back at the
too-familiar train car,
precise in its similarity
to every locomotive
that sped me from Ossining
to the city, and back again.
Will I ever return to Ossining?
The question sucked the air
from my lungs like a straw,
made my heart beat double-time.

Mom waved from the platform
waiting beside the man
I supposed to be
her new husband.
"Hello there," he called
in that fake kid-friendly voice
some adults use.
He reached for my suitcase,
as if I'd let
a stranger take it.
I swung the bag behind me.
He shrugged.
"You must be Bernice's daughter."
"One of them," I corrected,
walking straight to Mom.
"Hi, Baby," she said.
"I'm so excited you're here.
Ready?"

For what?
I focused on
cutting through the throng
to the local train station
and studying the subway maps
during the long ride
to a place in Brooklyn
I'd try to learn to call
"home."

DING, DING, DING

Slant is the only way I can tell this:

“Here we are” is the way my mother’s new husband introduced the Brooklyn brownstone I’d be calling home with him, a total stranger. His name was familiar, though—Clark, like the nice man who’d bought me ice cream once, except he’d been Clarke with an *e*. I smiled, thinking of him. This new Clark opened the door and out poured a chorus of unfamiliar voices. “Oh! She’s here!” I nearly slipped out of my nine-year-old skin, the noise startled me so. I’d have turned around to see who “she” was, but Mom nudged me forward, and ushered me directly into a wood-paneled room festooned with WELCOME HOME banners, pink streamers, and balloons bigger than my head.

The furniture was pushed against the wall, dance music blared, and busy feet already pounded the parquet floor. The ladies and half the men were decked out for the party in progress, and apparently, they couldn’t wait to start. It was fine by me since the whole thing was a surprise. Mom paraded me past this host of strangers, including my grandmother, nicknamed Mac. Who could say I knew her?

Grandma Mac had never behaved as expected. I nodded her way but refused to speak. *If you had helped us like we asked you to*, I thought, *my sister and I might still be together*. Forgiveness was not up for discussion. Next came cousins I couldn’t recall, new neighbors I wasn’t supposed to, and a twelve-year-old boy named Peter, plus his parents, the Ashfords—our Barbadian landlords who practically sang their hellos.

I met Clark’s sister, her husband, plus Ronald, Clark’s sixteen-year-old son, who Mom never mentioned. “Is he going to live with us?” I whispered. Mom shook her head *no*. “He lives with his mother.”

Good, I thought. I wasn't ready for another brother. I didn't want anyone trying to take the place of Ken or Brad.

We moved on to Clark's father, a man with startling blue eyes Clark didn't share. I sensed similarities, but I couldn't name them. None of that mattered in the moment, anyway. The person I most wanted to see wasn't there. "Where's Carol?" I asked my mother. "Carol?" Her eyes flickered a little. "She'll be here soon," she said. "But today's about you!" Clark nodded, prodding me across the room.

"You still haven't met the other children." There was a boy who tugged at a tie he was probably forced to wear, and a tallish girl. They both looked about the same age as me. I couldn't be sure. Anyway, these people were random to me, with one exception: the man my mother had married.

I was bored of the party and the clutch of grown-ups in the corner going on and on about a war in some place called Vietnam, saying how we hadn't heard the last of it. "Can I go see my room now?" I asked my mother. "Of course!" she said. "Turn left at the top of the stairs. It's the second door down, after the bathroom." I recited her directions until I found it, then stepped inside. Thank God, the walls weren't pink. I hated pink with a passion. The walls were white—boring! But that I could fix with Carol's help. The thought alone was enough to make me smile.

I stretched my arms out in this room large enough to have an echo! My room in Ossining could fit inside it twice. I lay on the bed and breathed in the comfort. A few minutes later, Mom called up to me, said "my" guests were missing me. How did they get to be mine? I don't even know these people. But a voice inside said, *Don't be like that. Your mom's trying to do something nice for you. Try spending a little time at the party she worked hard on.* So I pushed myself off the bed and headed back.

On the way, I got an eyeful of Clark's father in the hall, grinding up against my grandmother like they were lovers, until she shoved him into tomorrow and backhanded him across the cheek so hard the sound cracked the air. I'm surprised no one else heard. It must've stung, but all he did was laugh, like it was some kind of love tap, which made me wonder just how much the son was like his blue-eyed father, which rang a bell of worry about what kind of trouble we might be in for.

SISTER

Carol's life and mine
so achingly separate,
I rarely knew
the where of her days,
or what shaped them.

INHALE

The next morning, I could breathe, no inhaler needed. The partiers gone, Mom and Clark at work, I was finally free to listen to the whispers of the apartment. Mom let me skip school for a week to settle in, so I had plenty of time to explore this cavern of a room. The closet swallowed up the few jackets, pants, skirts, and dresses I owned. My T-shirts, underwear, and pajamas swam in a single dresser drawer and there were two more to fill. Could I ever?

The room suddenly felt lonely. I missed Brad and Kendall. And Grace. And Mom and Dad B. I missed—*Stop it!* I thought. *What's the point? I'm here, now. Everything will be just fine, especially once Carol gets here from Dobbs Ferry. And when will that be, exactly?* With Mom, *soon* could mean days or weeks, or months even. There was just no figuring her out. I headed for the bathroom, showered, dressed, and wolfed down a bowl of cornflakes.

I grabbed the extra house keys Mom had left and stepped outside, ready for some air. It wasn't all that fresh, but it was cool at least, and perfect for walking. I sauntered to the avenue to check out the neighborhood and found a beauty salon, pharmacy, small grocer, a newsstand, a laundromat, and—*bingo*—one of those little everything stores with candy in the window. Finally, a business that required closer inspection.

I pushed open the door, spotted three kids hopscotching through the aisles, rearranging things on the shelves, and shaking cartons. They juggled soda cans, then popped the tops to watch the fizz spray everywhere. One boy pocketed a Snickers bar, and I was not the only one who noticed.

"Get out!" shouted the store owner, a wizened old Korean gentleman. The kids sauntered to the door, in no particular hurry. One boy kicked over a display of chips, then stomped on a few bags until they burst. The girl with them giggled. "I said get out!" yelled the owner again. "I'm calling the cops, right now!" "Yeah, whatever," said one of the boys. He picked up his pace, barely.

> The girl grabbed a pack of red licorice. "I love these!" she said, tearing into the cellophane with her teeth. I stood open mouthed, mind racing. *Why aren't they running out? Aren't they afraid the police will catch them stealing?* One of the boys stopped a few feet away, backed me against a shelf of peanut butter and jelly. "What the hell you lookin' at?" he asked with a snarl. That's when I stopped breathing. My voice deserted me. I couldn't have answered if I'd tried.

When I was little, Carol taught me how to respond to a snarling dog, how to show no fear, but that didn't seem to help here. The boy stared me down until the girl walked over and tugged his arm. "Let's book," she said. "Yeah," said the second boy. "Come on, D. J. We've got better things to do." "Fine," said D. J. The three ducked out and vanished around the corner.

> Once I could breathe again, I raced back to the safety of the brownstone. Peter found me there, sitting outside on the top step, rocking back and forth, staring off into the distance. At first, Peter walked by, saying nothing, and opened the courtyard gate that led to his family's basement apartment. Something made him come back, though, to check on me.

"You okay?" He must've asked a bunch of times because I heard him yelling *hey*, felt a touch on my shoulder, and jumped. "Whoa!" said Peter. "It's just me." I worked to slow my breath and sat back down. "What happened to you?" he asked, stepping closer. I shook my head in silence, at first. Then, words and tears poured out of me in a rush.

> I told Peter about the candy store, the kids ransacking the place, the old man calling the police. "Then the boy slammed me against a shelf and scared me half to death. Nothing like that ever happened in Ossining. I didn't know what he was going to do next." "Never mind him," said Peter. "What did *you* do?" I shrugged. "I just—stood there."

Peter was quiet for a moment, turned aside so I could wipe away my tears without him watching, then told me to stand up. "What?" "Stand up," he repeated. I rose, legs still shaky. "Show me what he did," said Peter. "Go on." I shrugged, then nudged him towards the door of the brownstone and pressed him up against it, wondering if this was some sort of city game. "Okay," said Peter. "And where were his hands?" Peter was inches taller than me, so I reached up to place my hands on the door, on either side of Peter's head. He nodded. "All right. Next time, you just raise your leg, high, like this, and knee him, hard as you can."

> "Knee him?" "Yeah." "Really?" I could see Peter was becoming impatient. "Just do it!" I was thinking it over when Peter said, "Oh, forget it," and pushed himself off the door. Just as he stepped aside, my knee sprung up. "Hey!" said Peter, jumping back. "I said kick *him*, not *me*! I meant for you to show me, you know, in, like, slow motion, or something. I wanted to make sure you knew how to do it to somebody else, like that guy in the store. Sheesh!"

The whole time Peter spoke, he held his hands over his privates like they were still in danger, which made me giggle. "I'm outta here!" said Peter, racing down the stone steps. I stopped giggling long enough to say thanks, but by then, Peter had already ducked inside his family's apartment. Standing steady now, I took a few puffs of my inhaler and went back inside.

I took a second shower and put on another set of clothes so I could start the day again. I spent the rest of the afternoon in my room, reading and jotting down a few lines in my notebook until my mother got home. After hearing Mom go on last night about the lovely new neighborhood she had brought me to, I didn't want to spoil her picture by mentioning my afternoon's unlovely adventure.

TAG

I chase sleep,
but she is hard to tag.
Little Women
leaves my suitcase
to keep me company
until my eyelids
seal tight
for the night.

Notebook

Where's Daddy? He promised I'd see him more when I was back in the city. I haven't seen him even once. Maybe he's busy. Maybe he doesn't have our new number. Maybe he just forgot. Or maybe not.

MIDTERM HUSTLE

Four more days at the brownstone
to familiarize the bay window
with the curve of my spine
as I lean against a wall
finishing *The Diary of Anne Frank*
without interruption.
Four more days before
I'm registered
in the new school.
Their term's half over
and, lucky me,
I get to be out of sync.
Ain't nothing quite like
starting off behind.
Carol would understand.
I'd call if I could,
but kids in Dobbs Ferry
don't have phones.
Their house mothers do,
but only for emergencies
that don't include
missing your sister.

Day #1 in my new homeroom,
the teacher smiles,
a lie that says,
"You'll be just fine,"
but I'm nobody's fool.
In this new school,
my grade is studying geography
I've already been taught
and being tested on history

I haven't.
The mere thought siphons air
from my windpipes,
and experience tells me
a full-blown asthma attack
can't be far behind.
I scramble for my inhaler,
count to ten,
and pray to God
I never have to
switch schools
midterm
again.

Notebook

Okay, God. How do we fix this?
School is all I've got going here.
I have to do well.
Any ideas?

BFF

Meet my new best friend,
the library, where I spend
afternoons playing
a new game I have to win
called academic catch-up.

Notebook

Born here? Yeah, but now I'm a small-town girl.
This big city scares me. I don't think I'm tough enough
for this place. Guess I better learn how to be. And fast.

I wish Daddy would call.
He's sure been scarce since I moved back from Ossining.

ABSENTEE

By this point in my life,
I'd learned not to have
expectations. Still,
with my father only
a few short subway stops away,
his continued absence
came as a surprise.
I couldn't have guessed
it was Mom who made him
keep his distance until,
finally, one night,
on the telephone,
I overheard her begging him
to stay away,
something about
wanting to give
her "new family"
a chance.
Understandable,
I suppose—except
it was too bad
she hadn't bothered
to give me
the memo,
didn't let me know
I wouldn't be seeing him
for years.

OTHERWISE OCCUPIED

As much in a hurry
as Mom was to bring me home,
newspaper articles about
labor and education,
A. Philip Randolph,
campaigns of the AFL-CIO and
the NAACP,
plus memberships to
half a dozen
civic groups,
stole most of her attention.
Apparently,
being constantly
in the know
meant having no time
for me.

A DAY LIKE THIS

Clancy,
on a day like this,
I used to hide out with you
in the backyard,
tossing balls and sticks
you could find or fetch
long enough
for my arm to feel so sore
I couldn't concentrate
on my troubles anymore.

Notebook

I wrote a Christmas poem for Mom, put it in a nice card. I noticed the opened envelope on the kitchen table, so I knew she read it. "What did you think of my poem, Mom? Did you like it?" She said, "What?" like she didn't even hear me, then, "Oh! The poem. It was nice. Have you seen my keys? I can't remember where I put them."

Thanks, Mom.

Mom B. would have said something.

HAPPY NEW YEAR

Castor oil and New Year's Day
have nothing to do with each other
unless you're me and the shooting pain
in your right side has you writhing
on the sofa, and your stepfather is tired
of hearing you whine, since, according
to him, you just have a little tummyache
so he orders your mom to give you
two spoonfuls of castor oil which only makes
the excruciating pain radiate.

In short order, we bundled up and braved the cold
for an icy drive to the first hospital we could find,
where we waited unattended till an Asian doctor
noticed me. He didn't like the way I looked,
squatted in front of me, fired off questions like:
"What's your name?" "Where does it hurt?"
"For how long?" Then he turned to Mom.
"Did you give her anything for the pain?"
The minute he heard *castor oil*, he bellowed,
"Nurse!"
The doctor explained
my appendix could burst,
and if the poison spread . . . His face
said the rest.

Clark, Mister Know-It-All, sat silent.

The next thing I remember is waking in
a sickly beige hospital room with stitches where
the pain used to be, and a mess of bandages that

kept me from feeling them with my fingers.
I didn't have enough energy to sit up yet. Besides,
I was so groggy, the only sane thing to do was
close my eyes.

I woke again later, caught a few words whispered
by my nurse, something about how lucky
it is Mom got me to the hospital in time.
Fifteen minutes more, and seeing a doctor
would've done me no good. I kept my eyes closed,
but I was thinking, *Luck has nothing to do with it.*
My heart said it was God.
Down in my bones, I knew I was one of the sparrows
God keeps his eye on, and I was pretty sure
he was saving me for something. I just didn't know what.

SOUVENIR

Midwinter at the bus-stop, bare legs numb from the cold. Mom's stupid rule: *Don't wear pants to school.* I bounced up and down, desperate to keep blood flowing. At ten degrees below freezing, naturally the bus ran late. I graduated to a constant shiver, hopping from foot to foot.

> "That ain't gonna help," said a boy, approaching fast, three more kids in tow, looking none too friendly. "My name's Catch. Who you with, little girl?" *The trick*, I told myself, *is to ignore him.* I walked to the curb and craned my neck looking for that bus. That's when I'm hit with "You hear me talkin' to you?"

I whispered, "Sorry," which I suddenly was, and turned away, praying he'd just vanish. "I axed you, who you with?" Like he couldn't see I was alone. "Come on! You gots to be with somebody. The Third Street Gang? Fourth Street? Sixth Street? They're all a bunch of pussies, but still." The *P*-word made me flinch. "I'm not in a gang."

> "You gotta be shittin' me. Girl, you live 'round here, and you wanna keep on living, you gotta choose a gang for protection. What say you join us?" he asked. "We'll look out for you, won't we, Dee?" I figured she was the one who answered, "Yeah." Like that was good enough for me. "No, thank you," I said, voice like honey.

"Y'all hear that? 'No, thank you.'" He mimicked me, but so what? "Look here," he said, "Me, West, Rashad, and Dee, we'll just leave you a little souvenir to remember us by. Then maybe you can think about joining us later. How's that sound?" Certain I'm about to get off easy, I nod, never noticing West and Rashad coming up behind me.

West held me steady while Rashad kneeled down on the concrete. I wondered what he was doing, my limbs so frozen stiff, it took half a minute for the pain to make it to my brain. My scream should've shattered glass. I tried breaking free, but three against one is bad arithmetic.

I looked down through tears to find Rashad holding a lit cigarette to my calf. He grinned, pulled it away for a second, let Dee blow on it till the embers glowed, then jammed it back into the newly singed skin. When Catch saw I was about to faint, he said, "Okay. That's enough."

Rashad let the cigarette stub sail to the sidewalk, then stomped it out. He joined the rest of his friends already halfway across the avenue, laughing their asses off. "You have a good day, now," Catch yelled over his shoulder, and left me at the bus stop shivering, only not from the cold.

I balled my fists and wiped away my tears, mad at myself for being so easy to pick on, for saying *sorry* and *no thank you* like some stupid fool. *I should've acted tougher. I should've been ready to fight back. I should've*—"Stop it!" I said out loud. "It's over. Just make sure you're ready next time." The crosstown bus finally came and took me to school.

I made straight for the nurse's office, got the burn cleaned, filled with ointment, and covered up with gauze. I never told the nurse who did this to me because, as far as I was concerned, those kids were nobodies, not worth the spit it took to say their names. I thanked the nurse for bandaging my wound, went to class, and chalked the whole thing up to one hard lesson learned.

Notebook

Clark wondered about my bandage. I never hid my hurt. So why didn't Mom ask me what happened? What is it about dark and ugly things? She never wants to know.
Who taught her to play pretend?

God, why does Mom refuse
to see, or understand
the way things be,
the way things are
sometimes black-and-blue,
sometimes plain old ugly?

INITIATION

A gang on every corner
my mother chose not to see.
Those streets rumbled with danger
for me.

LIBRARY CARD

A magic pass
I used to climb into
other people's skin
any old time
I needed.

Notebook

I wrote a new poem today.
Tried to read it to Mom, but she just grunted
and changed the subject. Again.

I can't count the gin bottles in the trash. No more blackberry brandy.
That's a bad sign. Any day now, Mom will start talking to people
who aren't there, claiming she's seeing the Messiah.
One more week,
she'll be seeing Satan everywhere she goes.

Hey! Maybe if I put Satan in one of my stories, she'd read it!
Could be worth a try.

CONTAGION

Not quite eleven,
I was struck with the terror
of red, some steady issue
flowing from my body
inexplicably, unless somehow
I'd cut myself down there,
but on what?
Were there tiny blades
embedded in
the toilet tissue?
Were there razors
embedded in the stool?
Or maybe I'd contracted
some deadly, incurable disease.
God, please! No! I thought.
I'm too young to die.
When I went to my mother
to confess this bloody horror,
she sputtered up a laugh.
"It's your period," she said,
speaking a foreign language.
I was obviously perplexed,
so she explained,
but only after
more laughter.
And just like that,
my abject fear
morphed into fury.
I snatched the sanitary pad
she offered,
hurried to the privacy

of the bathroom,
and muttered to myself,
"Damn it, Mom!
What good are you?"

Notebook

I wish Carol was here. Every time I ask Mom why not, she coughs up junk about "red tape." If Sis was here, I could ask her about stuff. Like periods.

I hate these lumps on my chest. They're making my undershirts stretch, and when I run, I can't keep them from jumping up and down. It's annoying.

I don't know why girls want boobs. What a stupid word. I wish my body would stay the same. Boys at school are starting to look at me funny. And so is Peter. And so is—no. I must be imagining things.

I've been watching Mom. I don't like what I see. She's started talking to herself, again. Damn it!

God, I hope this stuff isn't in me.

Paranoid schizophrenia.
The words alone let you know
there's something wrong.
On the surface,
my mother looks normal,
but she lives in a world
occupied by people
no one else can see.
Me, I'm just fighting to survive
Sick-Mom's roller coaster ride till
Sane-Mom hops off at the end.
Sweet peace until that climb,
that loop, that fast drop
begins again.

DELIVERANCE

Desperate for stories
of outrageous adventure
to ferry me far from
my world and my mind,
I reach for my stash
of library offerings
where I'm fortunate to find
a weathered volume,
blue as the sea,
bulging with Viking lore
suited to me,
tales that can
sail me away.

NUTS

One late December, I woke at 3 a.m.,
teeth chattering and body shivering beneath
three blankets, which made no sense,
so I hopped out of bed to investigate.
My bedroom window was sealed tight,
radiator hot as an oven on kill.
I hustled into my robe and sprinted
first to the bathroom,
then downstairs to the kitchen
to double-check the windows there,
but found no draft sneaking in from either.
Next came the living room,
which was as far as I got.

The bay windows gaped wide,
inviting minus temperatures inside.
Sofa and chairs, smothered in vinyl,
were pressed against the walls, and
twelve painted saints smiled from glass jars
illuminated by burning candles placed
in a rough circle on the floor.
Flames licked the sides of each jar as wind
whistled through the room, sucking the
gauzy curtains half out the windows,
then blowing them in again. Pieces of
newspaper flapped and fluttered against
the polished top of the coffee table.

An eerie drone rose from the center of the room
where my mother stood humming and
swaying her body in a semblance of dance.
She whirled round and round in

her filmy peignoir, her eyes flecked
with wildness, her bare feet silently brushing
the floor, her mind in some private galaxy of thought.
I'm certain she didn't even know I was there.

I clutched a handful of flannel to my throat,
shivering as much from fear as cold.
Jesus, I thought. *What now?*
One by one, I slammed the windows shut,
then ran to Mom, hooked her around the waist
and forced her to stand still, though not for long.
She shoved me aside and went right back to dancing.

Clark was useless when Mom was sick.
He never got her help.
Daddy wasn't much better.
What is it with men?
Maybe this time I could get Daddy to step in.

I raced to the kitchen,
wrenched the telephone from the wall
and started dialing. Two rings down,
and my mother's strong fingers
dug into my shoulder from behind.

"Hang up," she said, her voice a steel trap.
"Just what do you think you're doing?"
"Nothing," I mumbled, not wanting to set her off.
"What were you *doing*?" I took a deep breath,
stiffened in case she had a mind to smack me.
"I was calling Daddy," I said, turning to face her.

"Look," I said, "I'm worried about you, and—"
"It's okay, honey," she interrupted, her voice
suddenly soft, purring almost. "I'm all right.

There's no need to worry. I'm just doing this for Him.
You'll understand some day. They'll all understand."

I didn't ask who "They" were, or "Him" for that matter.
I just let her pat me on the head, and I went back to bed.
Come morning, on my way to school, I stopped at
the nearest pay phone, jammed a dime in the slot
and called Mom's mother. I may have little to say to Mac,
but Mom's still her kid, after all.
When I described the candlelight,
the dancing in the freezing cold,
Mom's loopy language,
Grandma sighed, and muttered,
"Lord help us."
She agreed it was past time
to call the men
in white coats.

Notebook

Who needs to see the movie Psycho?
Just stop by our house.
Don't ask for popcorn, though.
We're fresh out.

DETAILS

Not yet old enough
to sign commitment papers,
me getting Mom into a hospital
could be a roundabout affair.
On the rare occasion
when I was on my game,
I'd ring up the local gendarmes
as Mom was busy trying to, say,
burn the house down with
roomfuls of lit candles,
while winter winds blew in.
Then they'd take her for
a seventy-two-hour psych-eval,
no signature required.
But if I missed that window,
and I had Carol's number,
I'd call her. She always knew
exactly what to do.
She'd find a grown-up,
sometimes Daddy,
but usually Grandma,
who'd do in a pinch.
We'd take Mom to
New York Hospital or Bellevue,
the loony bin we're all too
familiar with.
If no adults could be found,
Sis would sign the papers and say
she was eighteen.
(She looked it, anyway.)

Sometimes, it took two tries
to get the hospital
to keep my mother.
She could've won
a dozen Oscars
for convincing doctors
she was lucid as you or me.
Only after she started
spouting off in mangled Yiddish,
or responding to voices
no one else could hear
would they finally decide
to take another look.
Sometimes, the three-day hold
was the most we could get,
then Mom was out again,
until the next time.

Are those details enough?

On this particular occasion,
I'm home alone with Clark,
shut up in my bedroom every night,
happy to have books for company.

Weeks passed before
the doctors let Mom go
so the awful cycle
could begin again.

Every damned episode
wore another hole in my soul.

Of my mother's trips
to the madhouse,
you insist I recall details,
as if all I've done is casually forget.
You've yet to comprehend
the necessary truth:
I wadded up each episode
like toilet tissue, flushed it
as far down the drain as
memory's septic system would allow.
Don't ask me to remember
those details now.

COMMITTED

The Snake Pit is only entertainment
if you've never lived it,
never walked the halls
of a psychiatric ward,
squeezing past bug-eyed strangers
in oversized pajamas,
grabbing at your shirt cuffs
as if to pull you into
the psychic abyss they're in.
It's no place to have to leave
somebody you call Mother,
even if what connects you most
is pain.

Notebook

I hate hospitals. I hate visiting Mom in one.
The patients there all give me the creeps.
I still go, at least once or twice.
I have to, just so she knows
I'm not throwing her away.

THE VISIT

She slouched in the corner
near the gated window,
casually draped in
my mother's perfect skin.
My much-rehearsed grin
and tremulous hello
elicited the usual
drug-induced spasmodic twitch
routinely followed by
the catatonic stare.
Although, while this was rare,
now and again, my studied patience
amounted to more than
its own reward:
a moment of clarity,
the startling presence of someone
there behind the eyes,
a total recall lasting all of maybe
ten or twenty seconds,
but, my God!
It was heartbreakingly beautiful
to behold.

Notebook

A few weeks in the psych ward, and Mom is back home.
Good thing I didn't wait for Clark to get Mom to the hospital.
The last time she had a breakdown, I caught her running down
the street naked, and Clark wouldn't even call the police, which
left it up to me. He was too busy being embarrassed that she's
his wife. Leave it to him, Mom would never get the help she needs.

Thank God, this hospital stay was a short one. She seems to be okay.
For now. Naturally, she swears she won't stop taking her pills
this time, won't go back to the bottle. Old song. Same verse.

REUNION

By and by,
Mom got better and
Carol moved in after
more than a year.
Mom's "red tape" excuse
had grown pretty thin.
It never made
much sense to me,
but so what?
Sis was finally there.
Every day,
I got to watch
Mom and Sis
do this dance:
One would retreat,
the other advance.
Neither agreed
what mother love
should look like.

I'd imagined us
sharing a room,
laughing and talking
late into the night.
But Mom said
a big girl needs
her own space,
so Sis, aged sixteen,
slept down the hall
all by herself.
Mostly, though,
I didn't care.

The missing piece
to my puzzle
was here.

Two months in,
on Mom's February birthday,
after Clark had gotten her
good and drunk,
I heard some
sort of ruckus
and ran into the hall.
Next thing I knew,
Carol was being
rushed out the door
by Mom
with no time for
explanation,
only my sister's
whispered goodbye.

GONE

She must have a wand.
How else could my mother make
people disappear?

Notebook

Carol called today. She's staying with Aunt Edna for a while,
over in Manhattan. She still won't say why she left,
says one day, she'll tell me, face to face, whatever that means.

Mom won't tell me what happened, won't even mention Carol's name anymore. One minute Sis was here, then, poof—she was gone. What did she do wrong? I better watch what I say and do, or I might get kicked out, too.

There's something about the way Clark stared at me last night—made me shiver. Wish I knew why. I know one thing: I was glad when he stopped.

Mom's drinking again.
I saw her sitting up in bed, reading To Kill a Mockingbird,
a half-empty glass of dark liquid in her hand,
and a bottle of blackberry brandy on her nightstand.
I slipped into her room when she was at work and
poured what was left down the drain.
I don't even care if she gets mad.

GRANDMA SALLY

There's no checking your color
at the door when you're
encased in black skin.
I caught Mom reading about
the Freedom Rides
and was well-versed in the
horrors of lynching
long before puberty.
The ghost of Emmett Till hung heavy
from the time I was five.
So, at age eleven,
when Grandma Sally,
my mother's grandma,
asked my mother to send me South
for a visit, I flat out refused to go
even though it meant a break
from the madness that was home.
I was all for getting to know family,
but visions of me mouthing off
to the wrong white person,
or failing to step off a sidewalk
if ordered, or being dragged
off a bus because
I dared to sit up front
were recurring nightmares.
So, no, Mom, I told her.
Not going. Not ever.
Don't send me there unless
you seriously want me to die.

I never got to see Grandma Sally.
I'll just have to meet her

on the other side, where racism
has been excised
and justice is
common as dirt.

Notebook

Clark quit another job, the third since I moved in. When I came home from school today, he was walking around the house with a robe on and nothing underneath, unless you count that flagpole he was pointing in my direction. Ew!

I told him to get that thing away from me. He laughed.

Carol and I don't talk much. It's like we're a million miles apart. Sometimes it feels like we were sisters in another life. When we're in the same room, no one could be closer. When we're in different places, it feels like distance is all we have in common. It's a different kind of normal, when the foster system splits you up. You're connected, but not. Doesn't mean I don't miss her.

SIX O'CLOCK NEWS

Stomach growling,
I walked into the living room.
"Mom, when's dinner?" I asked.
She put a finger to her lips,
pointed to the TV.
A young man named James Meredith
flashed across the screen,
hedged in by snarling white men,
women, and even children,
celebrating their communal hatred
by pummeling this brown man-child
with eggs and epithets
I wasn't allowed to use.
Only National Guard troops
got him through the doors
of Ole Miss.
And what was all that
ruckus for?
Somebody colored
wanted to enroll
in a white university!
Deep inside,
I felt a burning
send my appetite
up in smoke.

Notebook

I'm black.
You don't like that, do you?

Liar.

Who's that I see
lying on the beach
with suntan lotion?
Is that you?

Yeah, I'm black.
But you like it.
Can't have it though.

It's all mine.

CLANDESTINE CHRISTMAS

Clark's son, Ronald,
came for a Christmas sleepover.
He was cute,
but too much older
to be bothered
spending time with me.

I was hyped up
for the holiday,
hoping for a two-wheeler.
On Christmas Eve,
Mom, acting weirder than usual,
insisted I go out
to wash a load of towels,
which was nuts
because the linen closet
was stuffed.
But she wasn't in the mood
for backtalk or excuses
so out I went,
in the snow,
full pout and all.

I cleaned and folded the lot,
and trudged back home
only to find Ronald with Mom and Clark
locked in their bedroom.
"What?" Mom sounded annoyed
when I knocked.
"I have the clean towels
you said you needed."
"Fine! Just leave them in the hall."

What the hell, I thought.
I tried to force the doorknob,
but it wouldn't budge.
I stomped downstairs
and waited in the living room.
A quarter hour later,
the three joined me.
Clark's lips were firmly zipped
for once,
and Ronald said nothing.
Mom placated me by suggesting
we open one gift apiece
before going to bed.
Ronald opened his first,
a watch with a band
like woven silver.
If that's what Mom got
her stepson, how much better
would my gift be?
Daddy's gift
would come late,
like always,
but it would come.
Meanwhile, the only thing
under the tree
with my name on it
was a lone, small box,
and I tore into the wrapping
like I was digging for gold.
Instead I found
Eau de toilette.
I looked from Ronald's watch
to my cheap bottle of scent
and understood perfectly

what it meant
to feel like
the stepchild.

I went to bed early
and took my sweet time
coming down the next morning.
Santa had nothing else
under that stupid tree
for me, which is why
my mouth fell open
when I found a Schwinn
parked in the living room.
"You better read the tag,"
said Mom, grinning,
"See who that bike is for."
You can guess the rest.

Notebook

Clark is staring at me now, all the time. I don't like it.
I'd tell Mom, but why bother? She'll just tell me it's nothing.

INTRUDER

"Come on!" I snapped,
impatient for the shower water
to warm. While I waited,
I checked my reflection in
the bathroom mirror.
That big-breasted girl
was a stranger.
I hated how my shirts hugged me,
how I jiggled when I walked,
how boys looked at me
like I was an ice-cream cone
with two scoops.
I climbed into the tub,
lathered quickly,
and stood beneath
the showerhead
eyes closed, enjoying
the feel of wet needles
pelting me. Then I froze.
"Who's there?" I asked,
sure I'd heard the door open.
I looked through the steam,
and made out a shadow.
"Get out!" I shouted,
covering my breasts.
"GET. OUT!"
The shadow quickly retreated.
It was Clark, of course.
I switched off the water,
reached through the curtain
and fumbled for a towel.

Maybe Mom catching Clark
gawking at me
while I take a shower
is what it's going to take.
Maybe then she'll leave him.

Notebook

Clark's taken to blocking my path
whenever I'm on my way up or down the stairs.
He forces me to squeeze by. "Oops," he says, like I'm stupid.
Like I don't know what he's up to. I hate this man.

I'm getting good at avoiding being in the same room with my mother's monster. Of course, she's an expert at pretending not to notice. I've stopped expecting anything different.

GIN RUMMY

I loved the sparkle
Mom got in her eye
whenever she was about to win
a game of gin rummy.
What I didn't like
was losing.
Mom would lay down
her winning hand with a flourish,
fanning the cards out
in front of her
like some show-off.
I'd slam my own useless
hand of cards
on the table, pouting.
"Aww," Mom would say.
"Don't be like that."
Then she'd offer to play
one more hand.
"I'll even let you win."
I'd suck my teeth, for show.
"Come on," she'd coo.
"Just one more hand.
Pretty please?"
The scripted scene
at its end, I'd cave.
"Fine. Just one."
Mom would giggle
and hand me the deck to shuffle.

On cue, Clark would bellow
from the living room,
"I'm out of beer!"

"Check the fridge,"
Mom would say.
Clark would grunt.
"Well, it's not doing me
any good in there, now is it?"
Mom would sigh and
leave the table.
"Be right back," she'd say.
"When you're done shuffling the deck,
go ahead and deal."
Then she'd go and do
Clark's bidding.
I'd be thinking,
You're killing me.
Why can't the bum
get his own beer?
Are his legs broken?
When Mom returned,
she'd mumble something about
Clark being a little grouchy
because he lost his job.
"Lost," I said once.
"You mean getting up and quitting.
Like he did the last time,
and the time before that,
and the time—"
"Never mind," Mom said.
And we went on playing,
but the sparkle in Mom's eye
was long gone.
Game over.

Notebook

Clark is driving my mom batshit crazy. He won't keep a job for more than a minute, which means she's got to work insane amounts of overtime to make up the difference, which is stressing her out, which is all the excuse she needs to dive into a bottle every chance she gets, even though she knows she's an alcoholic. And what does he do? Runs up a tab at the corner liquor store! God, do something! Please!

ESCAPE

I took to running
to Prospect Park and back
after school,
anything to get away.
Sometimes, Peter would join me.
"Race you," he'd say,
and every single time,
I'd beat him.
Guess I had more
chasing me
than he did.

REPORT CARD

Back from my run one evening,
I found Clark sprawled out on the sofa
per usual, doing lots of nothing
in front of the TV.
"Is Mom home yet?" I asked.
He shrugged.
"I'm watching the game."
He didn't even deign
to look up.
I checked the dining room,
the kitchen,
saved the bedroom for last.
I knocked but didn't wait
for an invitation,
just stepped into
the dimly lit room.
Once my eyes adjusted,
I spotted an empty bottle
on Mom's nightstand,
spotted the glass in her hand
before she tried to hide it
behind a stack of books.
"It's not what you think," she said.
Why do people always say that?
I glared at her, silent.
"I've been under a lot of stress lately."
She slurred her words.
"I just need—"
"Something to relax," I finished her sentence.
I'd heard it enough times.
"Yes. Well . . ." Mom's voice trailed off.
"I need you to sign my report card,"

I said, turning it over.
I watched to see if her hand
had started to shake
the way it always did
at the tail end of
a drinking binge.
She scrambled for a pen—
Not yet, I thought. *But soon*—
and quickly scribbled her name,
so she could hurry back to
sneaking her booze.
She was acting like
everything was A-okay,
like she wasn't halfway
to crazytown.
Again.

BROKEN

That night,
after Mom passed out drunk,
it happened.
I woke from a deep sleep
to find my legs parted
and Clark's tongue exploring
where no tongue
had ever been.
I tried to kick and wrestle,
but he had me muscled into place.
He kept licking and nibbling me,
and I screamed.

God, close your eyes.
I don't want you
seeing me like this.

Clark came up for air
long enough to laugh.
"Scream all you want," he said.
"Ain't nothing gonna wake
your mama."
Just to make sure,
he clamped his hand
over my mouth,
and that's when the tears came,
and I let them.
When he was good and done,
he got up, slung his robe
over his shoulder, and
sauntered from the room.
I gathered my strength and rose,

pushed all my furniture
up against the door,
and swore that bastard
would never
touch me again.

AFTERWARD

Breathe. Breathe,
I told myself. But I couldn't.
I ripped off my pajamas
and put on clean ones,
but what I really wanted
was to peel away my skin
because it was on fire,
like every inch of me
that he had touched
was scalded, and
it wouldn't stop throbbing.
Later that night,
I moved the furniture
from the door and snuck out
to the bathroom.
Three turns in the shower
and I discovered the limits of water.
There was no getting clean,
and I couldn't, for the life of me,
write the pain away.
I couldn't write about
any of it,
at all.

PROSPECT PARK SHOWDOWN

The next morning,
I slipped a butcher knife
from the kitchen drawer
and planted it underneath
my mattress, handle sticking out
far enough for easy reach.
Then I went on my usual run,
no jacket required.
I had enough rage to warm me.
When I was done tearing
through the park,
three gum-smacking girls
from the Sixth Street Gang
blocked my exit.
For years, I'd refused
to join a gang, even though
there was one on every street.
That made me fresh meat.
No surprise these girls wanted a bite.
Anyone who dared stand alone
elicited fear and hate,
each siphoning strength
from the other.
The gang's lead girl
drew a knife.
I caught the glint of a bottle
in the steel trash can.
I lunged for it, cracked the neck
against the can,
raised the jagged weapon high.

"Girls, you picked
the wrong damn day,"
I warned. But did they listen?
The three rushed me,
leaving a nasty six-inch gash
along one arm. The blood
ran freely, but I felt no pain.
I was still alive, for one thing,
and I wasn't the only one
left hurting.
When Mom asked what happened,
I gave her the lie she wanted.
"I bumped into a door with
a rusty nail."
Long ago, she'd let me know
she didn't want to hear
anything scary about
her neighborhood of choice.
"We'd better get you
a tetanus shot,"
was all she said.
"Grab a towel," snapped Clark.
"I don't want you bleeding
in my car." I withered him
with one look and said,
"Blood in your ratty old car
would be an improvement,"
which shut him up.
On the way to the hospital,
he switched on the radio.
"Talk that Talk"
by Jackie Wilson was playing.
I said, "How about you let
Jackie do all the talking?"
Mom looked at me funny,

since I'd never given Clark
much lip.
My scowl let her know
I was just getting started.

Notebook

Mom told me to start packing. Since Mr. Useless can't seem to hold a job, we can't afford this neighborhood anymore. She found a cheaper place in another part of Brooklyn. Perfect. So does the new address come with a less screwed-up family?

I keep thinking of Carol today, the strange way she left.
For a moment, I close my eyes, and I can see
the smirk Clark wore as Sis went out the door.
Did he touch her, too? Is that what she wants to tell me?
She's not welcome here. Mom has certainly made that clear.
I haven't seen my sister in months.

If Clark hurt Sis, she'd have gone straight to Mom and—
of course! Mom didn't believe her, probably called her a liar.
Why else would she show Carol the door?
Mom only sees what she wants and—God knows why—
she wants Clark in her life, or in her bed, at least.
Did Carol and I both pay the price?

JUST

Just arrived on a new street.
Just another midterm move.
Just another blur.

WHAT TIME FORGOT

Schools
and street names
are gone.
Blame it on
the Mad Hatter,
or the madness
of my every day.
Either way,
the specifics
climbed a horse
and rode out of town
long ago.

Notebook

Gin bottles are turning up again.
And we're off!
Next stop, paranoia.
Shit.

Still having trouble sleeping, and I refuse to cry.
I pack my tears away.
Tears belong to people who are weak,
something I swear to never be again.

THANK GOD FOR CHUBBY CHECKER

Music wafted through the window,
the lyrics stealing
straight into my heart.
"I'm just about at
the end of my rope."
The August heat
added to the fire
in my bones,
and no amount of
ice cold pop
could cool
the seething inside me.
The annual block party
brought mournful strains of
Garnet Mimms
& The Enchanters' "Cry Baby."
I took one look at
Mom and Clark
tossing back shots of
brandy and Johnny Walker Black,
transporting them to
nowhere I wanted to be,
and I cursed under my breath,
ducking outside
without giving notice.
"Nowhere to run to, baby."
One door-slam later,
and I closed my eyes,
pretending to be
the lone dancer
in the middle of the street,

stomping out my hatred of Clark
while doing the Mashed Potato,
wadding up my anger at Mom
and drowning it in
Smokey Robinson and the Miracles'
"Tracks of My Tears."
Sweat pouring off me,
I surrendered to
the happy beat
of Chubby Checker,
who helped me
plant my feet
in the moment,
and twist, twist,
twist the night away.

Notebook

Funny how, no matter what, morning comes. How weird is that?
The sun makes no sense when everything inside
is shadow.

RECORD KEEPING

My spiral notebook bulges
with poems and prayers
and questions only God
can answer.
Rage burns the pages,
but better them
than me.

FRIEND SHIP SAILS AWAY

I'm sure I made friends in Brooklyn.
So why can't I
remember them?
Or the schools I attended?
Or the teachers I loved?
Instead, my
Brooklyn recollections
are all of Mom
filling her days
with blue thoughts
and blackberry brandy,
of her recurring trips
to the psych ward,
of me tap-dancing past
the local gangbangers
until I couldn't.

And then there's all the
unwanted memories
of Clark—always Clark,
thrusting his ugliness at me,
raking my
woman-child flesh
with a greedy hunger
in his eyes,
and him clawing
at my innocence
with filthy fingers
until there was
little room left
in my memory
for much else,

which is a shame, really,
because the friends
I do remember
were splendiferous.

BIRTHDAY ASSESSMENT

Thirteen was a year
of revelation.
I turned out to look
not so bad, thank God—
despite my detestable
horn-rimmed glasses.
Then there was my natural
try-and-stop-me stubbornness
and wicked-as-all-get-out wit,
attractive qualities
on their own.
My sister—damn her—
turned out to be voluptuous,
while I was merely cute.
It hardly seemed fair,
but, for the record,
by thirteen,
I ended up the tallest
in my family, a proud fact
which, at times,
made me insufferable.
I often called Mom Pygmy.
Believe me, she was not amused.
But, the way I figured,
since she'd saddled me
with this oversized proboscis,
I had every reason to tease her
limited stature.
We all have our crosses
to bear.

CRIMINAL INTENT

2 a.m.:
I woke to voices clanging like
a discordant gong.
Clark's deep voice
in menace mode:
"Get off my back, woman!
If you don't want to
work overtime, don't!"
Then Mom: "I wouldn't have to
if you'd keep a job
for more than ten seconds,
always talking about how
'The Man' treats you
with no respect, as if
you'd earned any."
It was an old argument
that went nowhere.
Like always, I pulled the pillow
over my head, but this time
there was a scream
and the sound of something
bump, bump, bumping
down the stairs.
I grabbed the butcher knife
from beneath my mattress
and sprang into the hall.
Clark swayed dangerously
at the top of the stairway. Alone.
"Where's Mom?" I demanded.
Before he could answer,
I leaned over the banister behind him,
saw her crumpled motionless

on the floor below.
"Mom?" I called.
"Mom! Talk to me!"
When she didn't, I thought
That's it, and moved toward Clark
in what felt like slow motion.
His back to me,
I raised the butcher knife
in a daze, about to swing when
Mom's voice
cut through the haze.
"Don't, honey!" I froze.
"Mom?"
"I'm okay," she said.
"Really, honey. I'm fine.
Don't do this, baby. Please.
He's not worth it."
Clark turned to me,
trembling.
"I'm sorry. I didn't mean to—"
"Get out!" I shouted.
"Get out, now!" and for once,
Clark acted like he had some sense,
raced down the stairs
and slipped out the door.

My eyes burned into him
as he bolted,
and I thought of something
Mrs. B. used to say:
"God don't like ugly."
You see this, God, right?
I know you do.
I know it.

I ran to my mother and,
for a while, we wordlessly
held each other.
My breathing slowed,
and I began to shake,
staring at the deadly weapons
connected to my wrists,
the pair of hands that nearly
killed a man.
How could they be mine?
"Oh God, oh God, oh God,"
I whispered. Still wobbly,
Mom fought to sit up,
took me in her arms,
and cried the tears I wouldn't.

Notebook

After all this time of keeping him away, Mom must have called Daddy. He came to pick me up, said I'd be staying with him for a few days. She'd call the school and tell them I was sick, so no worries there, but I wasn't sure about leaving Mom. She looked at me steady, clear-eyed, and said, "I'll be fine now. Trust me." Something about the way Mom said it let me know she meant it. I packed an overnight bag and left. Before I did, I set that butcher knife on her nightstand.

REVELATION

Daddy picked me up
for a quick and quiet drive
to his apartment.
When he arrived,
I stood stiffly for his hug,
still uncomfortable
being touched.
Besides, I hadn't seen him
in ages.

He ushered me into
the mess of his
two-bedroom flat,
clothes strewn everywhere,
dirty dishes in the sink,
nothing in its place.
Who'd want to live here?
I thought about when
he'd said he didn't know how
to care for little girls.
I finally believed him.
Even so, if he'd kept
Carol and me,
Clark could never have—

No point in going there.
I didn't even want Daddy
to see that thought on my face.
I'd keep this ugly secret
from him.
There's nothing he could
do about it now, anyway.

"Excuse the mess," he said,
clearing space for me
on the sofa.
"I'll straighten up a bit,
then you can go to sleep
on the pull-out."
I nod,
offering no help.
The way I figure,
he could use some practice
taking care of his
not-so-little girl.

DISORIENTED

I woke, startled that
there was no knife
underneath my mattress,
then remembered
I was at Daddy's place.
My shoulders relaxed
as I rubbed my eyes,
grateful
for a little peace.

COMFORT

The next night,
we silently shared a booth
at a neighborhood pizzeria,
and later sat on his sofa
watching who knows what
stupid show on TV,
something that would
make me laugh.
Instead of plying me
with questions
I wasn't ready to answer,
he reached for me
and, after a moment's hesitation,
I let his arm
make itself at home
around my shoulder,
squeezing love
through every pore—
his silent assurance
there was enough of it
to fuel me
no matter what.

Notebook

Too bad I couldn't stay with Daddy longer. Clark's back again, like nothing ever happened. So he's sleeping on the couch. So what? I'd be happier if he was sleeping in the street. That's where he belongs.

Why is the devil
back in my mother's bed?
Leave it to him,
she'd be long dead.
One thing, though:
I bet he now knows
not to mess with me.

SHOTS FIRED

Altogether,
1963 was a terrible, horrible,
no-good, very bad year.
One November evening
I came home from school
to find my mother
clutching a photo
of John, Robert, and Ted Kennedy
flashing those
impossibly white teeth.
Below the photo, the words
"Dear Bernice,
Thank you for your support
of the Democratic Party."
Mom delicately ran her finger
over John's image,
and emptied out
every tear in her body.
I knew just enough about
JFK and hope
to join her.

Notebook

Carol's got her own apartment. She called as soon as she moved in. She says it's not very big, only a studio. But still. It's hers. Seventeen, with her own apartment! It's up in the Heights, not far from Aunt Edna and Uncle Abe. She's working as a cook to pay for it. Good thing she's learned how to. I don't think her customers would like that raw oatmeal and buttermilk she used to feed me! Anyway, since she's underage, the restaurant's paying her under the table, until her eighteenth birthday.

I've been thinking, maybe I should go stay with her. No. *I can't leave Mom. Not as long as she's with Clark.*

TURKEY TROT

Thanksgiving brought with it
new notes of grace.
Clark left. Wrote himself
out of our story.
That's all the ink
I'm willing to spill
on the matter.

Notebook

I went to the library today, returned five books. I thought about not returning A Tree Grows in Brooklyn. *I want to read it again. I read it twice, already. In some ways, Francie's just like me. We both know the color of hell by heart.*

REST

I count down the days of quiet,
enjoy the calm
before the next storm
Mom is sure
to invite.

Notebook

I was never happier to leave a place.
No matter where we end up, Clark won't be there!
I packed up my room before I was even asked.
The moving truck couldn't come fast enough.

A GOOD GOODBYE

I sealed the last box in my room,
shoved it out into the hall,
eyes sweeping walls,
dresser, bed, each holding
the imprint of my fear.
Good riddance, I thought
and slammed one door,
ready to walk through another.
New neighborhood,
new school.
New Mom?
The night before,
she'd gathered every bottle
of gin and brandy
hidden in the house
and poured the contents
down the drain.
"I'm leaving this place behind,
and the drinking along with it."
Silence was the only honest answer
I could offer.
"I mean it, this time," she said.
"I hope so." I was past the point
of pretending to believe.
Still, I'd heard of such things
as miracles.

BOOK FOUR

1963–1966

"Tamar put ashes on her head, and tore the long robe that she was wearing; she put her hand on her head, and went away, crying aloud as she went."

—2 Samuel 13:19

My narrative's a puzzle.
What's next and next and next
I couldn't say.
The moments, hours, days
a jumble.
The only thread connecting them
is me, and even then
the thread is frayed—
the break, at most,
a hair's breadth away.

THE HEIGHTS

Money thin as tissue,
the issue before us
was what we could afford.
Solution: become boarders
in a rooming house.
The stay would be brief,
Mom swore.
Three months, maybe four,
long enough to pocket
rent and security for
a proper apartment.
Until then, Mom and I,
galaxies apart,
would share one room, one bed.
Great new start! Not.
Moving from two stories
to two nightstands between us,
squeezed was a word
too big to fit
the miniature space,
the new place we were
supposed to call home.
Night One, walls pressing in,
I ran out to the stoop for air.
Amsterdam Avenue
was waiting there,
apartment buildings
close enough to kiss,
liquor store on one corner,
Holy Ghost Revival Center
on the other, barber and
beauty shop in between,

and the sweet stink
of Sherman's Barbecue
tickling my nose from next door.
Mom joined me outside,
said we should try
barbecue for dinner
and my stomach
growled on cue.
Still, my thirteen-year-old self
stood there, eyes closed
for a minute or two,
breathing out Brooklyn,
breathing in
Washington Heights.

Notebook

I'd like to miss the bay windows
in that Brooklyn brownstone
where I could curl up
and read for hours,
or miss those planked
maple-wood floors
slick enough for me
to slide across
when the mood hit.
I'd like to miss
the curving banister
that I would sniff
when it was newly polished
so I could catch that whiff
of lemon scent.
But how can I miss
window, floor, or banister
when that house flooded with
an ocean of ugliness
that practically
swept me away?

MATERIALIZED

Clark finally gone,
I get to see Daddy
whenever I please,
even though I'll be living
a few extra miles away.

SHARING THE LOAD

Carol lived closer now,
a short shot up Amsterdam,
twelve city blocks away,
but I didn't see her much.
She was in no hurry
to share the same air
Mom breathed.
I almost squealed
when Sis turned up in Bed-Stuy
one weekend, while I
was visiting Daddy.
He was practicing his violin
as she tiptoed in,
his eyes closed, like always.
She lowered herself to the floor
beside me, and we both
listened for a while,
holding hands.
Then Carol, who dreamed
of being a singer like Della Reese,
started humming along
in her smooth contralto.
Daddy's eyes flew open
at the sound of her voice.
"Come here, you!" he said,
giving Carol a one-armed hug,
before swinging his violin
back to the familiar
crook of his neck
and kiss of his chin.
Sis and I busied ourselves
in the kitchen

devouring my private stash
of lady finger grapes (my favorites!)
while scrounging enough
from Daddy's cupboards and fridge
to manage sandwiches for lunch,
and teasing poor Daddy, who
couldn't boil an egg.
When I was sure
he was out of earshot,
I told Carol about Clark
and that night.
She clenched her fists.
"That bastard!" she hissed,
hoping Daddy hadn't heard the outburst.
She took me by the shoulders
and leaned in close, her eyes afire.
"Don't. Ever. Tell. Daddy,"
she whispered.
"I won't. Don't worry," I said.
"He'd find that bastard
and kill him," said Carol,
which, by the way, we both agreed
was no more than Clark deserved.
Still, neither one of us wanted
to have to visit our father
in prison.

NEW DIGS

The new apartment we found
was two doors down from
the grandmother I had no use for.
Mom reminded me Grandma was
the only mother she had and asked
if I could please consider giving her
a second chance to love me.
I was not so inclined; however,
God kept pestering me about
this thing called forgiveness, which
seemed ten kinds of impossible.
I was still mad at her for leaving
Carol and me in foster care,
and mad at God for letting her.
Still, I did see Grandma
trying to make amends
with gifts and sweet treats.
I eventually got the drift.
Maybe it was time
to heal the rift.

DC-BOUND

Washington, DC
started calling
the minute Daddy said
we'd be driving there to see
Aunt Esther and Uncle Howard.
My overnight bag
bulged with jeans
and rumpled shirts
I could iron
once we got there.
I sat in the living room,
tapping my feet
till the phone rang.
"Sorry, honey," Daddy said.
Great. Here it comes, I thought.
"Something's come up.
We won't be going, after all."
I bit my lip,
ripped open my overnight bag
and spilled the contents
on the floor,
then stomped out the door.

Notebook

Facing exams on topics my last school was just getting into and my new school already finished. God! Might as well call me Catch-Up, since that's my middle name.

YOU DON'T SAY

I quickly learned how little
I knew Grandma Mac—
her preferred moniker.
She came from poor stock down South,
sharecroppers, to be exact, and she'd
had to quit school early on to help
support the family. She'd hardly had time
to learn to read, but determined to
expand her knowledge on her own.
I can't remember ever seeing her
without a book nearby. Next to
the lamp on her reading table, she kept
a Webster's dictionary so she could
look up any unfamiliar words
and, though stubbornly proud
about most things, she saw no shame in it.
"Never be afraid to admit there's something
you don't know or understand," she told me,
and I suspected she meant more than
the vocabulary she amassed like treasure.
I started dropping by Grandma's for visits
and one-on-one conversations, and I'd
slip her a page or two from the years
that were lost between us, so she
could slowly read my story.

PINEAPPLE SURPRISE

After my grandmother
discovered my fondness
for pineapples,
this sweet knowledge became
a weapon she wielded
whenever she felt the need to
express her love and regret.
She'd go to considerable trouble
to bake a pineapple upside-down cake
from scratch, just for me,
then would gleefully watch
as I set aside my
adolescent aloofness
long enough to devour several
honey-soaked slices like
someone starving.
Sharing was not required,
unless I so chose.
Those sticky cakes never
quite made up for Grandma's lack
of physical affection,
but my belly happily accepted
the substitute.

The Mystery of Memory #3

Think food,
and nourishment
comes to mind,
but we all know
it's so much more.
One bite of baked pineapple,
and my tongue sticks
to the roof of memory,
gluing me to the last moment
I savored a slice of
pineapple upside-down cake
at my grandmother's kitchen table.
Each tangy morsel
transports me,
and I am thirteen again,
relishing a culinary treat
sweet with the hours
it took Grandma to make
this Maraschino cherry–topped,
gooey offering of love.

NEW SCHOOL

They called it junior high,
those middle years
between childhood and
oh-God-I'm-practically-a-grown-up.
The school term had already started,
but that was nothing new.
Thanks to frequent changes of residence,
I had lots of experience
at midterm party-crashing.
I smiled a lot and acted like
I belonged while in class,
then snuck off to the library
to read my way through lunch,
sneaking bites of egg-salad sandwich
when no one was looking.
Surviving is almost easy
if you have a strategy
and a copy of
A Wrinkle in Time.

Notebook

My life is like musical chairs.
Every time the music plays, I have to move.
I wonder if I'll ever get to stay in one place
longer than three or four years.

THE LANDSCAPE

Once again,
I ended up near water—
the Harlem River
barely a block away from school
made me think of the Hudson
till I chased the thought away.
No point hankering after good times
long gone.
I kept my nose in books,
dodged broken glass on sidewalks,
veered past winos holding up lampposts,
and avoided bullies as best I could,
not because I was afraid of them,
but because I half suspected
my slow-burning anger,
simmering beneath the surface,
made me more dangerous
than I wanted proof of.

ROAD TRIP

Daddy ruined me with frequent
road trips, mostly to DC
to see his older sister, Aunt Esther,
and her husband, Howard.
I don't remember ever
staying for long,
but any ride with my Daddy
was a sweet adventure,
and the destination
was never
the point of it all.

APPLESAUCE

My father was
the baby of the family,
spoiled rotten by his sisters.
Aunt Edna, my favorite,
would often whip up
homemade applesauce
whenever we happened by,
teaching me
not all applesauce
is the same.
Her tongue-tickling,
tangy blend of
smooth and chunky apple yum,
was kissed with
just the right amount
of cinnamon and nutmeg
and an extra special
secret ingredient
Aunt Edna once whispered
when she was sure
I was sound asleep.

IN THE BACKGROUND

You'll notice,
if you haven't already,
I no longer talk
about my mother,
and anger
is not the reason.
I've little time for that.
Instead, I've entered
into the realm
of simple mistrust.
I've learned that Mom
is not to be counted on
for more than room and board.
Emotional support
is hardly on the table,
and any steadiness I might need,
I have to look for elsewhere.
Schizophrenics and alcoholics
are not known for their
reliability.
I've been tested, though,
and already know
on my own,
that I'm a survivor.
I can live on the hugs
of my father,
the smiles of my friends,
the boundless faith
of my sister,
and the dreams
God whispers

in my soul.
If Mom needs me, though,
I'm here.

ENGLISH CLASS

I was smart
and a smart-ass.
Truth be told,
you couldn't tell me much.
Foul-mouthed kids
warned me
not to think I was "all that"
just because
I said *ask* instead of *axe*
and got great grades
in English.
I didn't much care
what they thought,
as long as I got to write
book reports
and compositions,
or any other homework
that let me
lose myself in words.
Somehow, I knew writing
could take me places.
Even my teacher
told me so.
Still, there was no
getting around
one unfortunate fact:
writing was
a lonely business.

SIDESWIPED

Note to self: no more
writing in my notebook
while parked on the stoop.
One day, I made that mistake,
and the neighborhood number runner,
bored with taking bets, I suppose,
showed up out of nowhere,
interrupting me.
"Hey, girly. What you doing?"
he asked, as if
it wasn't obvious.
I sighed and looked up.
"Writing," I said,
expecting that to be
the end of it.
He rolled his toothpick
from one side of his mouth
to the other,
a gold incisor gleaming
when the sun slipped in.
"Writing, huh?
Writing what?"
If I tell him, I thought,
maybe he'll go away.
"Poetry," I said.
"Damn, girl!
Why you wasting your time
writing that?
Poetry ain't gonna
get you nowhere."
To keep the sharp blade
of my tongue

from slicing him
into fine strips,
I pressed my lips together,
barred my words
from escaping.
"What you gonna do
with 'poetry'
when you grow up
and gotta pay the rent?"
I slammed my notebook shut
and stomped inside,
grinding my teeth
until my jaw throbbed
from the pressure.
I climbed the five flights,
muttering to myself,
"Some grown-ups
should damn well
wash their mouths out
with soap."

CAROL'S MANTRA

My sister used to say,
"The world is going to hear
from the Grimes sisters,"
usually as a way
to punctuate
the latest
poem or story
I read to her
when we were
visiting Daddy.
"Yes, sir," she'd say.
"The world is going to hear
from my baby.
You just watch."
Her pronouncement
was a hope,
a prayer,
a promise,
a good word I could
tuck into the pocket
of my heart
to be reminded
of my potential
whenever the world
seemed bent
on convincing me
that I had
no such thing.

KINDRED SPIRIT

A girl named Jackie saved me.
We met in the school library,
two glasses-wearing geeks
who the other kids
called stuck-up.
Not much of a writer,
Jackie did match me book for book,
searching for a better future
than either of us saw
in the mirror
of our neighborhood.
That's it, I decided.
From now on,
I'm only hanging with
other kids
who dream.
I believed in Jackie,
and she believed in me.
Funny how far
that can take you.

BULLY ON PATROL

A stout student
named Brenda
stalked me.
I never did figure out
what made her itch
for a throwdown.
Each day, she managed
to bump into me,
or poke me in the arm
accidentally on purpose.
Every infraction
was followed by
a cackle.
I'd bite my lip so hard,
it nearly bled.
"You really need to
leave me alone,"
I warned her,
again and again.
"Trust me," I said,
"You don't want
to make me mad."

Of course,
I was already heated
when Brenda
turned my switch to boil.

Fists flew,
and they were mine,
and honestly,
I don't remember much

except seeing red
and punching, punching,
punching Brenda in the face
until her usual smirk
ran sideways,
and she lay
sprawled across
the sidewalk,
her blood everywhere
and me trembling
atop her,
wondering
what the hell
just happened.

Notebook

I woke screaming again last night. I wish it was because of some stupid nightmare. It's worse. The possibility of ending up like Mom, of having that sickness in me—it's too much.

God, please don't let insanity be
my inheritance.

SOLVED

No one at junior high
ever bothered me again.
I was safe, but terrified
of my own power.
Sometimes I'd look at my hands
like they were the craggy claws
of some monster
terrorizing a small town
in a horror movie,
and I'd shiver.
Pent-up anger
proved a dangerous thing,
and I could no longer allow it.
From that day forward,
if someone or something bothered me,
I voiced it on the spot.
No more messing around
with emotional dynamite.
Not for me.

JUNE 1964

Joy is in short supply.
God, don't you see?
Past, present,
darkness everywhere,
sinking its gnarled roots
deeper into the world:
Mom's mind,
Clark's heart,
the white-hooded devils
setting the South on fire,
turning black men
into torches.
Freedom Summer exposes
this twisted sister
called America.
I press down my own pain,
cry instead for Chaney,
Goodman, Schwerner,
only they can't hear me
or anyone
anymore.

COUNTEE CULLEN

Everyone has a nexus,
that place on the map
of your life where
who you were born to be
is clearly marked.
For me, that was
104 W. 136th Street—
the Countee Cullen Library
in Harlem.

I was thirteen
the year my father
signed me up
for my first reading,
a gathering of young poets,
though, as it turned out,
none was as young as me.
I was excited,
leading up to the day.
That all went away,
however,
the moment
my name was called.
I'm still not sure
how I stood.
My ashy legs,
thin as toothpicks,
were an earthquake
of movement,
and the fingers
that held my notebook
trembled like

an aftershock.
I stared at my hand
as if it didn't
belong to me,
then looked to my father
for deliverance,
this being
his bright idea.
"I can't do this,"
I whispered.
But my father
spoke away my fear
with a powerful incantation:
"You'll do marvelously.
Just keep your eyes on me."
And, like magic,
my breathing slowed,
and I rose
to the occasion,
reading my poem
in a clear voice,
my father's faith
and loving gaze
holding me steady
as promised.

GRADUATION

Daddy's uniform of choice
was black beret, sports coat,
white shirt, dark slacks
and baby-soft leather loafers.
By my count,
only one other time
had I seen my father
in suit and tie,
and that was in
his wedding photo.
This let me know
my graduation
from Stitt Junior High
was important.
When my name was called
for special recognition
I looked toward my teacher
for explanation.
"Go on," she whispered.
I inched my way to the stage,
swallowing hard with every step.
The principal handed me
a copper medal
engraved with
an old-fashioned feather pen
sticking out of an inkwell,
her way of telling me
to keep on writing.
It was the first time
I truly believed
it was possible to burst
from happiness.

Notebook

At the library on a Saturday, which is fine, but I'm supposed to be on my way to the planetarium with Daddy. Another no-show. Some excuse about a rehearsal that slipped his mind. He's probably somewhere gambling. Whatever.

Last weekend, I got to see Carol. We were both visiting Daddy at the same time. She seems to be doing okay. She just moved into a bigger apartment. Now that she's eighteen and officially a grown-up, she finally gets paid out in the open, and got the raise she asked for.

I told Sis about Convent, this church I've started going to. I met a girl there named Debra. She's a junior usher and I'm in the junior choir. Something tells me we're going to be good friends.

CONVENT AVENUE BAPTIST CHURCH

Black churches
always have names
wide as broad-brimmed hats,
I don't know why.
I liked that *Convent*
was relatively short.
My mother rarely attended.
Back then she was busy
studying the Torah
with her friends Scott and Ruby,
the only black Jews I knew.
I went to bar mitzvahs and bat mitzvahs,
and knew "Hava Nagila" by heart.
And don't get me started on
the wonders of potato latkes, lox,
and pickled herring!
I didn't pick up any Hebrew
or understand much
about being Jewish,
but frankly, any religion
that kept my mother
on the straight and narrow
was fine by me.

Convent reminded me warmly
of the Buchanans
and the church in Ossining
they took me to.
Once again, I found my place
in the choir.
Singing hymns brought me

close to God when he
seemed absent from
my everyday.
And through
my new friend Debra,
church brought me the family
I was missing.
For that alone,
it became easy for me to say,
"Hallelujah!"

A BREEZE

1.
Except for math,
high school started out a breeze.
In ninth grade, I came home excited,
though as a teenager, it was necessary
to feign nonchalance.
My English teacher, Mrs. Volcheck,
had marked my latest story A+
calling it "the best thing she'd read
in a long time."
As soon as Mom got in from work,
I planned to share the news,
forgetting for a moment
who my mother was.
The A+ barely garnered a grunt.
As for any interest in reading my story . . .
"You know," she said, eyes firmly fixed
on the six o'clock news,
"Writers are a dime a dozen."
And just like that—*bam!*—
she slammed my heart
in the door of her words.
When will I ever learn?

2.
I refused to let my mother
see me fight back tears.
She didn't deserve to hurt me
and know it.
"I'm going to Deb's," I said,
and slipped out the door
before she could object.

I half-ran the few streets
between my building and hers,
then climbed the three flights
to Deb's apartment,
cursing with every step.
It was Debra's mother, Willie Mae,
who answered my knock at the door,
Bop, Debra's tailless Manx cat
not far behind.
"Hi, honey," said Debra's mom.
"Hello, Mrs. Jackson.
Is Debra here?"
She cocked her head,
listened to more than my words.
"No, sweetie, but you come on in."
When I hesitated, she grabbed my hand.
"What's the matter, sugar?
Come sit down and tell me." So I did.
To her credit, she never once
bad-mouthed my mother.
"Well," she said,
"not all moms are the same."
Bop meowed in agreement,
and rubbed up against my leg, purring
before padding from the room.
Willie Mae fell silent for a moment,
then looked deep into my eyes.
"You are a very talented young lady.
Don't let anyone tell you different."
Which, of course, was what I needed—
that and the blanket of love
Willie Mae wrapped around me
with her hugs.

REDIRECTED

There was always a two-ness
about my mother,
some shadow of a twin,
an alternate persona,
one forever at arm's length,
the other not.
At times,
there was a flicker
of light in her,
a flame burning
bright enough
for me to feel the heat.
The flame would rise when
neighbors or co-workers
were in need.
She'd prepare
a hearty soup for them
from scratch
or bake a batch of cookies
to lift their spirits.
For such kindnesses,
that mother was beloved
by untold unfamiliar people
beyond our door.
On them, she lavished
the attention
I had once
been hungry for.
Oddly,
her redirected affections
made a certain kind of
sense to me.

Apparently,
my sister and I had made
the colossal mistake
of not being
strangers.

Notebook

Not much laughter these days.
I'm home alone; Mom's back in Bellevue.
Damn it to hell! Sorry, Lord, but
it's ridiculous! She'd be fine—
if she just kept taking her pills,
if she just stopped DRINKING.
Two things! That's all she has to remember.
Why can't she do that?
Why?

And once the doctors let her go,
she'll want to start over again, you know,
move to some new where—
I'm not sure when.
Give me a hint, Lord.
IS THERE GOING TO BE AN END*?*

THE SOLID ROCK

Desperation drove me from bed some Sundays,
        Through this world of toil and snares
hungry for the hymns that rocked me like a baby.
        If I falter, Lord, who cares?
Off to Convent I went on a scavenger hunt for hope,
        Who with me my burden shares?
and each week, I left with a sliver of it in my pocket,
        None but thee, dear Lord, none but thee.
enough to brave the darkness at home, once again.

LET AULD ACQUAINTANCE BE FORGOT?

The holidays barely over,
February was bloody
with bombings in Vietnam,
which should have provided
more than enough hemoglobin
for anyone keeping record.
Yet, just yesterday,
El-Hajj Malik El-Shabazz
slammed into eternity
when shots rang out
in the Audubon Ballroom,
a whistle away from
my sister's apartment.
Winter weather
isn't the only thing
keeping me
numb with cold.
I keep waiting for the world
to wake up wiser,
to choose life
over the grave.

MATH MADNESS

Algebra should be
ranked under
fatal diseases.
One more equation,
and I'll die.

TERRA FIRMA

The poem I wrote
for earth science
was a good idea, I thought:

Silently,
in the hush of morning,
in the busy hum of day,
in the belly of night,
rocks, greedy for touch,
rub together beneath the soil,
shifting side to side,
waking the ground above.
Backyards ripple,
hills rumba and roll,
trees bend, break,
skyscrapers shimmy, shake,
riverbeds sway,
spilling waters every which way,
and roads split as if
pinking shears had snipped
the fabric of the earth
and ripped the rocks
that started it all.
After the shudder, a sigh,
and the ground grows still again,
pretending to be terra firma.
Until the next time.

Now who wouldn't want
a poem like that?
My science teacher, apparently.
"I'll need a proper report

on seismic activity tomorrow,
Miss Grimes," he told me.
I didn't say what I was thinking.
Profanity is frowned upon
in school.

Notebook

Last night, Daddy's chamber group performed at Carnegie Hall, in a small room they rented. Carol was there too, right next to me.

We'd never seen Daddy dressed up in a tux, or seen him half as nervous. When he crossed the stage, clutching his violin, I could practically feel him shaking. It made me think of that time at Countee Cullen Library, when I was the one doing the trembling. Now, it was my turn to give him *courage, to hold* him *steady with a look of love.*

SMALLS PARADISE

Summer brought a little piece
of nightclub heaven,
fine dining in a space
once sharing the same
rarefied air as the Cotton Club:
Smalls Paradise, the first hot spot
owned and operated by a black man—
a flashy footnote in the annals of jazz
I knew nothing of on the day when
my father and I crossed its threshold.
For me, it was the dimly lit musical shrine
I had begged Daddy to take me to so I could
sit at a dinner table that nearly kissed
the stage, and witness my sister shine
in her silk-gowned glory, singing
"Nobody Knows the Trouble I've Seen,"
and bringing down the house.

Notebook

I went to my first art exhibit! It was by black painters my dad knew from reading The Liberator, *like Tom Feelings and Leo Carty.*

I've never seen anything like it, all those drawings and paintings of people tan and yellow and black as me, and every one of them, some kind of beautiful. I just kept staring and feeling—good, I guess. Daddy told me who each painting was by, but he mostly just watched me and smiled.

I think Tom Feelings was my favorite.

Black so beautiful,
beaming from
white paper,
white canvas,
paint gone wild
with color.
Who knew
we could glow
even
in the dark?

THE COPA

Going to the Copacabana
was never on my list of things to do.
I was too young
to understand the appeal.
But my father, sporting shirt and tie
for the occasion,
escorted me there
for a celebration
of the one and only
Lorraine Hansberry.
I'd never seen *A Raisin in the Sun*,
and couldn't tell you
if the cast was present,
but I clearly recall hearing
the voice of Paul Robeson,
an actor and singer
I'd seen on TV and read about
in *Ebony*.
Riding up the elevator
on the way to the festivities,
I noticed a dark,
caramel-colored
smallish man,
eyes bigger than quarters.
When the elevator doors parted,
he was swarmed by
finely dressed crowds
adorned with adoration.
"So very, very honored to meet you,"
blathered one woman,
pumping his hand
too long for comfort.

"Daddy," I whispered,
"Who is he?"
"A famous author," said my father,
with unfamiliar awe.
Hearing that,
I stared at the man
long and hard,
memorizing the contours
of his face.

The gala at the Copa
went on for hours,
punctuated by songs, speeches,
and the majesty
of lithe-limbed black dancers
snaking across the stage.
Of all I saw and heard
that evening,
I was most struck with
this single revelation:
not all stars in the firmament
were white.

GARMENT DISTRICT

Grandma Mac
had a close kinship
with style.
When she offered
to take me shopping
in the Garment District,
the only answer was yes.
A tenth grader
heading into fall,
it was high time for outerwear
more fashionable than a peacoat,
and Grandma knew
exactly where to find it.
We tramped in and out of
designer shops on Seventh Avenue
until my feet cried *mercy*.
I groaned, done for,
when Grandma insisted
"Just one more store."
But I followed her into
another boutique.
"Try that on," she said
spotting a swing coat
with a collar so furry-soft
it practically purred.
I slipped it on
and grew two inches,
suddenly confident
in my beauty.
"We'll take it,"
my grandmother told the sales clerk,
and I sashayed out,

sore feet forgotten.
Grandma Mac certainly knew
a myriad of ways to
rack up brownie points.

TRIO

Girls. Girls are aplenty,
but *girlfriends* are a special lot.
Debra, Gail, and I called ourselves—
you guessed it—
the Three Musketeers.
Debra was my bestie,
and Gail possessed
more natural literary talent
than I was blessed with.
I made up for the difference, though,
with confidence enough to squander.
One afternoon,
we three dressed up
in our finest rags
to help Gail's boyfriend,
a fledgling photographer
in need of a portfolio
to display his considerable skills.
Debra and I ripped off our glasses,
and we three posed for portraits
in the park
(me in my new coat!),
then hung from
a vertical pole
in the middle of a subway car,
swinging round it gleefully,
pretending to be
professional models.
In other words,
we hammed it up, yo!
And those photographs?
Oh, my God! Portraits
of joy.

COURSE CORRECTION

The first year at William Howard Taft
shot by like a bullet.
I cleverly surmised
the second year
would be the same.
By then, we'd moved to the Bronx,
up near the Grand Concourse,
for who knew how long.
Bone-tired of switching schools,
I put my foot down,
told Mom she could
move us to Mars,
for all I cared,
but I wouldn't be
changing schools again.
Surprisingly, she gave me
no argument.

My tenth-grade subjects
provided very little challenge,
except for math, which I decided
was clearly the work of the devil.
English, on the other hand,
would be a cakewalk.
When Mrs. Wexler,
my new English teacher,
handed back our first
graded compositions
of the year,
I was nearly fifteen-going-on-
you-couldn't-tell-me-nothin'.
Hence, I was smugly prepared

with a smile of victory,
certain of the perfect score
awaiting me. After all, was I not
the most brilliant writer in the class—
nay, in the entire borough
of the Bronx?
When the paper
landed on my desk,
scarred with the letter *B*,
I nearly choked.
"Excuse me," I said, barely civil,
"there seems to be some mistake."
"How so?" asked Mrs. Wexler.
"Well, I've never gotten less than an A
on any composition. Ever."
"Really?"
She was clearly unimpressed.
"Class, please take out
Catcher in the Rye
and read silently."
I reached for my book,
thinking her quite rude
for cutting off our conversation.
"Not you, Miss Grimes,"
said Mrs. Wexler.
"I need to see you for a moment."
And she waved me over
to her desk.
Offensive paper in hand,
I went forward.
"Miss Grimes," said she,
once I stood before her.
"If this were written
by anyone else in this class,
it would have garnered an A.

However, you clearly have
a talent for writing
that you are not yet using
to the full.
If you want an A from me,
Miss Grimes, you'll have to
apply yourself, dig in, and do
the very best writing
of which you are capable—
and nothing less.
Understood?"
I managed a nod
and a bit of a stutter.
"That will be all,"
said Mrs. Wexler.
"You may return
to your seat."
Flabbergasted,
I wandered blindly
for the remainder
of the day,
in complete
and utter
shock.

COIF

The barbershop
between 147th and 148th streets
on Seventh Avenue
was owned by Debra's father, Doll.
Great news for me,
since being his daughter's friend
meant getting haircuts for free.
I paid though, in other ways.
South African singer
Miriam Makeba's
close-cropped coif
is the sleek 'do I imagined
when I posed in the mirror.
My dad loves Miriam and her music,
has her album covers face-out
on his living-room shelves
and a poster of the
high-cheekboned black beauty
smiling from his wall,
all the reason I need
for wanting to look just like her.
This I explain meticulously
the first time I go to Doll's shop for a trim.
He nods, like he's listening.
He asks before he starts,
"You sure you want it that short?
'Cause if you're sure,
I can give you what you want."
"I'm sure," I say,
never doubting my vision
or his ability to make me
as beautiful as I want.

Then he grabs his clippers
and dots the floor with my tight curls.
When I see my free trim, I gasp
and drag myself home,
still dreaming of Miriam Makeba,
but looking more like
a skinny black boy with a buzz cut,
ready to join the Marines.

Notebook

Debra saw my first buzz cut and covered her mouth,
but not before a few giggles escaped. I rolled my eyes.
"Aw," she said. "Come here."
She ran her hand over my head.
"It doesn't look that bad—Baldy."
"Shut up!" I said.
Then we both burst out laughing.

Notebook

"Happy 15th Birthday, Baby." *Daddy's cards are corny.*
He got me another book, this one about
the Mali Empire. If he keeps giving me
books about African kingdoms,
I'm going to change my name to Queen.

BLACK MAGIC

For some of us,
childhood photos
are rare.
Years in and out
of foster care
fosters a sense of
invisibility.
Our lives are routinely unrecorded,
perpetuated
however innocently,
by unthinking parents
and other performers of
a dark art—
withholding proof
of presence.
We have no
cartons bulging with
faded report cards,
sheets of construction paper
messy with
finger-painted handprints,
no dimpled or freckled images
lovingly plastered across
refrigerator doors,
or obsessively created
memorabilia of any kind.
We pretend not to mind
this fractured version
of peek-a-boo:

Now you see us,
now you don't.

Notebook

The Black Panther Party is starting to look real good to me.
To join, or not to join? Haven't made up my mind.

Debra has a boyfriend. I'm not ready yet.
Raul, this 'Rican boy in my class, smiles at me
every chance he gets. He's fine, too—brown and beautiful.
I bet he'd laugh if he heard me call him that.
It might be nice to be with him, but . . .

I can't stand the thought of anybody touching me.
Don't know when that'll change. If ever.

I told Debra about Clark, what he did to me. Some of it, anyway.
She asked how come I still believe in God. What kind of question
is that? How could I not? If it weren't for him, I wouldn't even be
here. I'd either be in prison, or the grave.

Notebook

Little by little,
I hear God telling me
to let the anger go.
Clark is gone.
Mom is who she is.
I can't change her
or Grandma.
All my anger does
is get in the way
of my dreams.

GREASE PAINT

Roger Furman,
a New York theater director,
got me hooked on theater.
My father introduced us, of course.
(Who doesn't that man know?)
Roger led a small troupe in Harlem
and invited me to join.
Visions of being Sidney Poitier's
leading lady, or maybe
sharing the Broadway stage
with Harry Belafonte,
put stars in my eyes.
After that,
there was no keeping me away
from auditions.
This was it:
I decided I was going to be
a writer/actress.
No question.

LES BALLETS AFRICAINS

My sour experience in ballet class
back in Ossining
gave me mixed feelings
about going to the ballet.
But my father was insistent.
He assured me I'd like
the special performance
he had in mind.
He might as well have been
talking about the Milky Way,
because black women doing pirouettes
was a vision
out of this world.
Their grace, their beauty,
the talking drum rhythms
that reached into my soul
reignited my love
of dance.
This was it.
I was going to be
a writer/actress/dancer.
No question.

HOLD EVERYTHING

A slightly familiar lady
who knew my mother
from way back,
stopped me on my way
from paying a visit
to my grandmother.
She trapped me
with the usual
adult chit-chat:
how much I looked like
my mother,
how much I'd grown
since she saw me last,
blah, blah, blah.
But then she got to
the main event,
asking what I wanted to be
when I grew up,
as if I wasn't
grown enough already.
"A writer/actress/dancer,"
I rattled off,
and she chortled.
"Wait!" I said,
having almost forgotten
how much I loved
being in the choir.
"I'm going to be the first
writer/actress/dancer/singer,"
I announced
(not knowing Maya Angelou
had already beat me to it).

"Honey,
you're going to have to choose
one or the other,"
said the woman.
I didn't see why,
but I was taught
not to argue
with my elders.
When I saw my father
the following weekend,
I repeated the conversation
to hear what he had to say.
"Don't worry about choosing
right now," he told me.
"Go ahead and explore
whatever art form interests you.
There's plenty of time
to decide on your specialty,
and once you do,
you'll discover you can use
everything you've learned."
Hot damn!
Give that advice-man
an Oscar!

Notebook

Daddy says I can be
whatever I want.
Carol says I can be
whatever I want.
Debra says I can be
whatever I want.
Her mom says I can be
whatever I want.
Mrs. Wexler says I can be
whatever I want.
They're right.
Everybody else
is lying.

BLACK ORPHEUS

I loved the sound
of conga drums
in that grand old Brooklyn theater
built back in the 1930s,
offering its faded velvet curtains,
chipped paint, and dull cornices
with barely the reminiscence of gilt
by the time I saw them.
But the sound that bounced
off the cathedral ceilings
still swelled to fill the hall,
each note round and golden.
And there I sat beside my father,
below the balcony
surrounded by a small group of black folk,
enjoying the glory of
ebony-hued Brazilian dancers
swaying across the movie screen
as Daddy's favorite old film,
Black Orpheus,
loomed larger
than any I'd ever seen.
Much of the story
set against Brazilian Carnival
was over my head, but
the parade of costumed dancers
in sun-soaked colors
and elaborate masks
held my attention.
At one point, I turned to my father
to profess my awe at what I saw,

but found him sound asleep,
as usual.
That man could fall asleep anywhere,
even standing up.
Mom used to say my father
wasted his money on movies,
said he could sleep more cheaply
at home.
He missed most of the film,
but stirred at the end when
Mongo Santamaría's band
hit the stage,
beating the congas so hard
Daddy's heart woke
to the vibrations.
Later, I asked him
why he'd taken me to this movie
if he couldn't even stay awake,
apart from the concert that followed.
He said what really mattered
was that I have a chance to see
all there was of black beauty
and music and magic in the world.
Otherwise, what would I weave
into my stories?

Notebook

Daddy knows everybody, I swear. Today, he took me to meet John Oliver Killens—at his house! He wrote this famous book of essays called Black Man's Burden, *giving white people a piece of his mind. Daddy had him autograph a copy for me. My first signed book ever!*

MICHAUX'S

Mention Harlem
and the Apollo is what
often comes to mind, but
Daddy introduced me to
another entertainment venue:
National Memorial African Bookstore
or, as everybody called it, Michaux's,
its exterior busy with posters
and signs like:
"Knowledge is power
and you need it every hour."

I followed Daddy through the door and,
like Alice, slid down a magical rabbit hole.
Eyes too wide for words,
I gazed at the walls and walls of books
sandwiched together:
The Souls of Black Folk, *Black Boy*,
Maud Martha, *And Then We Heard the Thunder*,
books signed by Eartha Kitt, LeRoi Jones,
and Langston Hughes, a local.
Surely, the neighborhood library
was jealous!

From the corner of my eye,
I spied a staircase leading—where?
"What's there?"
I asked Mr. Michaux, pointing.
"Go on down and see," he coaxed.
Daddy nodded, letting me know
it was okay to explore.
I trod carefully, step by step,

down into a dimly lit cavern
of floor-to-ceiling metal cases
bulging with even more books.
I roamed the narrow aisles,
gingerly tracing the
delicately bound spines
as if each was
a book-shaped diamond,
the name of each author a ruby:
Zora Neale Hurston, John O. Killens,
Rosa Guy, Gwendolyn Brooks,
Henry Dumas, Chinua Achebe—
hundreds and thousands
of beautiful books by and about
people who look like me,
stories from the African Diaspora
my father spoke of passionately.

For more than an hour,
I devoured a page here, two pages there,
easily squeezing between bookcases
crammed so tightly,
no claustrophobic
could survive the adventure.
As for me, I knew I'd found
a place to call home
for the foreseeable future.
When I finally let Daddy drag me away,
I left Michaux's with a single thought:

My books will be here, someday.

Notebook

I spent the weekend with Daddy. We didn't go out anywhere, since it was raining, but I didn't care, except for the food part. I just ended up making us eggs and toast until I got sick of it. For dinner, I talked him into ordering pizza. Might as well give up thinking he's ever going to learn to cook.

MY BLACK ME

My father fed me
Invisible Man,
Native Son,
No Longer at Ease,
Black Man's Burden,
and the more I read,
the madder I got,
and I already
had reason
to scream,
but my father
kept me dreaming
of what words
I might bring
to the world.

ROOMMATES

I don't try sharing
my life with Mom anymore.
We're just roommates, now.

Notebook

I got to hear Daddy practicing Messiah *on his violin last weekend. He's getting ready for the holidays. Man, I wish I could ride around with him as he travels all over Jersey and DC, sitting in with the violin section of different orchestras, playing the "Hallelujah" chorus. Maybe next year I'll ask if I can tag along.*

EASTER EVE, 1966

There was a ripple in my soul that night.
A push. A pull. It's difficult to describe. There was
a wordless something that poked and prodded,
and made sleep impossible. And then it came,
a harsh telephone ring, piercing the air, bringing
the unwanted explanation: On the Jersey Turnpike,
on the way home from visiting his Cousin Isabel,
Daddy was in a terrible crash, smashed into the median.
My father's MG now nothing more than an accordion.
What was left of him lay in a hospital, dying.
I can't tell you what powered my body, how I managed
to dress, fold myself into the taxi next to my mother, or
even find breath as we sped to the emergency entrance.
We learned what room he was in, raced to the place
we didn't want to be. A doctor stopped us at the door,
told us to prepare ourselves, as if we could.

My eyes were as confused as me, not knowing where to focus.
There were countless tubes crisscrossing the hospital bed,
revealing bits of the broken body that was supposed to be
my father. He was unrecognizable beneath the endless swaths
of bandages and bruises. And the sounds! The noises!
The beeps, the mechanical whistles, and the drone of the
oxygen machine threatening to shut down between breaths,
at any moment, it seemed. That was enough to send me screaming
from the room, but I remained. Useless. Tearless. Stunned,
leaning against a wall, staring at my father until I couldn't.
Stumbling into the hall, I found Carol there, and we clung
silently, holding each other up, and my thoughts spun
and they spun and they spun a web empty of words,
except for two: *oh, Daddy!*

MARKING TIME

1.
The pacing began.
Hope and I
pounded the pavement
between visits
to the death room.

2.
The weeks turned
like a mad spinning wheel,
weaving worry
into despair,
a useless thread.
Each day,
there was less of my father
to hold.

3.
Morning by morning,
he wept,
tears the only language
left to him.

4.
Five weeks in,
the truth revealed
was unrelenting
in its sadness.
The *if* of his survival
a stunted thing.
His beautiful brain

a wreck, a relic to be
relegated to the past.
No more symphonies,
no more sweet violin solos,
no more holiday "Hallelujah" chorus.
Lord, my sister and I prayed,
Take him fast.
The adults reprimanded us,
understanding nothing
of our love.

5.
One morning,
I found my mother
at his bedside,
caressing his cheek,
and whispering promises.
"You come through this," she said,
"and we'll give it another try."
It was too late for what she wanted,
but I could see her heart breaking.
I slipped into the room and laid a hand
on her shoulder.
Why do some people
wait too long
for everything?

6.
Week six,
my father fell asleep
while I was home in bed,
a hard answer
to a hard prayer.
Was there mercy too, Lord,

in the end?
If there was,
my Daddy woke up
in heaven.

FINDING FAULT

Daddy's death unequivocal,
I came home from the funeral
with space in my brain
for questions.
Why was he driving
so late at night?
Why didn't he sleep over
in Jersey
at Cousin Isabel's
and drive home
Easter morning?
We all know—knew—
his penchant for
nodding off
anytime, anywhere,
which is why he avoided
getting behind the wheel
when he was sleepy.
Why'd he do it, this time?

A phone call to Cousin Isabel
was slow to provide an answer.
She hemmed and hawed and dodged,
until I pressed her.
"He'd promised to see you
Easter morning,
and he refused
to break his promise,
said he was done
with all that.
I told him to stay here,

get some rest,
call you in the morning,
but he wouldn't listen."

Isabel heard my voice
clogged with tears.
She would've hugged me
if she could.
"It's all my fault,"
I whispered.
"No! Don't go there, honey," said Isabel.
"This was your father's decision,
no one else's,
and it would kill him if—sorry.
I mean to say,
he wouldn't want you
to blame yourself."

My voice went into hiding,
so I hung up the phone.
Cousin Isabel said
all the right things.
Still, that night,
a sliver of guilt
pierced my heart.

Notebook

Mom started drinking again. I didn't notice until after
we got back from the funeral.
Not now, Mom. Please!

"How are you doing?" Mrs. Wexler asked when I went back to school. She knew my father was my best friend. I shrugged because, really, what could I say? I wish it was my mom 'cause that would have been easier? You can't say things like that. Not out loud.

I don't care what
Stokely Carmichael says.
I may be black,
but I don't feel
powerful
at all.

NEWS ROUND-UP

There's something on the news
about an unmanned spaceship
headed for the moon,
but I can't take it in.
Tears make everything
blurry.

Notebook

I came home yesterday, still numb from Daddy's passing. I found a novel in my book-bag I didn't put there. That Mrs. Wexler, always slipping me a surprise. She really keeps me going.

The novel was Another Country *by James Baldwin, some author Mrs. Wexler says I should know. I turned the book over and saw the photo of the author. My mind was a little foggy. Still, I knew I'd seen him before, but where was—oh! At the Copa. The man in the elevator. A famous author, Daddy said. Wow. I get it now.*

We had a good time that day, Daddy, didn't we?

CANDLE IN THE DARK

The Prophet
warmed my pocket.
I carried that tea-stained,
dog-eared paperback
everywhere I went.
The sheer muscular light
of Khalil Gibran's language
made me want to be him
on the inside,
made me long to
chisel away the dark,
wielding sharp,
light-bringing words
of my own.

Notebook

Mom's wigging out again,
seeing people who aren't there.

Lord, if this thing
turns out to be in my DNA,
I'll scream.
Have mercy, Jesus.
I don't have the energy
to go through life
like a loon.

WORDS TO LIVE BY

"No matter what's going on
with your mother,"
Mrs. Wexler told me,
"focus on your studies,
on your future.
That's your job.
Your father
would say the same,
wouldn't he?"
I nodded, then she
put me to work
writing another
essay.

Notebook

I missed my last homework assignment.
Some book I was supposed to read for a report.
Mrs. Wexler called me into her office. I didn't even bother to try to hide my pain.

"This too shall pass,"
my teacher tells me.
I'd suck my teeth
and turn away,
but I don't because
Mrs. Wexler told me
she's a Holocaust survivor,
and I read
The Diary of Anne Frank.
Somebody comes back
from that,
you have to believe
anything is possible.

MIXED GRIEF

The pain of losing my father
could not be quantified or even hinted at,
though the realization that he was free of pain
brought a flicker of pleasure that
no measure of grief could destroy.
But I missed the lyric strains of
that violin he played so well.
It hurt to imagine a universe
devoid of his ministering melodies.
Mom never understood:
she needed their healing
more than most. But
she hadn't earned my sympathy.
My thoughts were on me
missing a father forever gone, off
creating cantatas in heaven,
and praising God
in *pizzicato*.

Notebook

Daddy wasn't much of a dancer. He was better than somebody with two left feet, but barely. Something I read in The Prophet *tonight made me think of that. It was a chapter on death, and it said,* "And when the earth shall claim your limbs, then shall you truly dance."

Daddy, are you dancing now?

ICE QUEEN IN SUMMER

Dressing for the day,
I found the pristine pair
of milk-white ice skates
Daddy lavished on me
last Christmas.
I retrieved them
from the closet floor,
ignored the sharpness
of the blades,
and grabbed, them, clinging,
bringing them to my bed,
where I sat, caressing the last gift
my father would ever
have the chance
to give me.

The Mystery of Memory #4

Where do memories hide?
They sneak into
Hard-to-reach crevices,
and nestle quietly until
some random thought
or question
burrows in,
hooks one by the tail,
and pulls.
Finally, out into the light
it comes,
sheepishly.

Who would imagine what
the mere sight
of ice skates
might open?

Watching ice dancers
compete on TV,
I flash to the skates
my father had gifted me.
But why?
Why'd he buy them at all?
So odd.
I had never skated.
Or had I?

A call to an old friend
woke visions of me

clinging to the rails
at Wollman's Rink
in Central Park,
tentatively pushing off onto the ice,
holding Debra's hands
for dear life
while she
spun me dizzy,
reminding me
of her Olympic dreams;
the exquisite joy of glide,
of spin, of jump,
feet finally fitted
in those magic
silver-bladed boots
made for flying.
And there, flashes of
sipping hot cocoa
on the sidelines,
inaugurating my
lifelong tenure
as spectator—
so many moments
tucked away
in the crevices
of my mind.
All. That. Time.

Yes.

This is the mystery
of memory.

SUNDAY MOURNING

I sat in the meticulously
polished pew, waiting for
I don't know what.
The church service
had long ended, yet
there I sat, discovering
the meaning of lethargy,
gazing listlessly
at the pipe organ,
which stared back, offering
no answer.
Why'd my father,
the one parent
who knew my heart,
have to die?
Debra slid in next to me,
laid her head on my shoulder,
and shared the silence.
Or did I imagine it?
Either way, my best friend
was a comfort
who never once demanded
I hurry my grieving
and move on,
which is why
I didn't mind
her seeing
my tears.

FELONY ON FALLOW GROUND

Back home from a neighborhood
basketball game, I ran to my room
to rip off my sweaty shirt and change into
something dry, but first I stopped
to jot down a few thoughts
in my spiral notebook, which was
nowhere to be found. I checked my desk,
my dresser drawer, the floor,
even underneath the bed, just in case.
Anything was possible, right?
And where were my other notebooks?
The ones that usually lined the small shelf
attached to my headboard?
I'd filled pages and pages over the years,
half of them smudged with tears,
fingerprints, Kool-Aid stains, and jelly
from sandwiches I stuffed down while writing.
Where'd they go? And where was my medal,
the copper one from junior high?
I went to find my mother to see if she knew,
found her in the kitchen, weaving drunkenly—
a familiar sight since my father's funeral.
"Mom, have you seen my notebooks?" I asked.
Was that a smile on her face?
"Yes," she said. "They're in the trash
along with all the other garbage
cluttering this house. I'm sick of it."

I stood stock still, forced myself
to go on breathing, felt the blood rush

from my head, down through my arms,
on out to my fingers as they clenched.
I felt my arm draw back, muscles taut
and ready to pound that sick, smiling face
until every tooth went flying, but
a single thought caught me in time.
She's not well. Just look at her.
My arm dropped and I ran.
I checked the wastebasket in my mother's room,
the trash can under the kitchen sink,
the bin in the bathroom, my room—everywhere.
I tore out the front door,
ran to the street praying,
Please, God. Please!
Let the garbage truck be late,
just this once.
But—no.

I dragged myself back in,
took a few puffs from my inhaler,
then whirled round my room
yanking open dresser drawers,
and tossing handfuls of clothes
on my bed.
I added shoes to the pile,
then schoolbooks
and the novels from Mrs. Wexler—
everything I'd need
to leave.

A voice inside
whispered urgently:
You cannot blossom
in this soil.
I knew it was true.

I dove into the closet,
hunted for my duffel bag,
stuffed it with
everything that mattered,
then—

Where am I going?
Where the hell am I going?
I dropped to the bed,
clawed the cover,
and clenched my teeth.

Jesus! Get me out of here!

I closed my eyes,
waiting.
Praying.
Behind my lids,
an answer finally appeared:
Carol.

Tears were a nuisance
I couldn't be bothered with,
so I wiped them away
with a back hand,
finished packing,
and phoned Sis to tell her
I was moving in.

Notebook

I dropped by Mrs. Wexler's office after lunch. It was great to see her after the summer. Mom's back in the hospital, which I told her. I also told her about moving in with my sister, and how Carol always let me wake her up in the middle of the night so I could read her a poem. Mrs. Wexler smiled. "You're on your way," she said. Then she asked me a question she'd asked before. "What do you want to do with your life?
What kind of books do you want to write?"

I thought about Demon, the darkness of that closet;
I thought about Clark, his sleazy black heart;
I thought about those girls in the park,
who scarred me for life, and the gang on the street,
who branded me with that cigarette;
I thought about the giant hole in my mother's soul
when alcohol and her mental illness took over;
I also thought about Carol, who took care of me
the best she could, whenever she could;
I thought about Daddy, who poured into me
the history of our people, and encouraged me to explore
all that the world of art had to offer;
I thought about the Buchanans, who made me part of their family;
about Debra, who loved me like a sister; about Willie Mae and Doll,
who embraced me like their own;
I thought about Mrs. Wexler, the hardest teacher ever—
the best, too. That's when I knew.

"I want to write books about
some of the darkness I've seen,

real stories about real people, you know?
But I also want to write about the light,
because I've seen that, too.
That place of light—it's not always easy
to get to, but it's there.
It's there."

EPILOGUE

Time unwinds faster than a slipknot
when the string is pulled.
It's one year since moving in
with my sister,
two since Malcolm X
was shoved into eternity.
I attend a celebration of his life
at a school in Harlem.
Debra offers to join me,
but I'm on a solo mission.
I settle in the front row
just as the program begins.
The first speaker
takes the stage, has his say,
then exits the auditorium early.
"Mr. Baldwin! Mr. Baldwin!"
I call, sprinting after him,
"Can I see you for a minute?"
I wave my spiral notebook as I run.
He pauses outside a classroom,
cocks his head in that familiar way
I've seen him do on TV.
"Mr. Baldwin!" I manage, breathless,
"I'm a writer, too.
Could you look at my work
and tell me what you think?"
He nods, ignores my crossed-out words,
and missing commas,
reads my rough poetry,
cover to cover,

then writes his name and number
on the back.
He looks me in the eye,
one serious writer to another.
"You call me," he says.
And I do.

Photo ©: David Flores

This photo was taken at the Langston Hughes House in Harlem, marking for me a triumphant return to the first place I called home.

AUTHOR'S NOTE

A memoir is a tricky business. Unlike an autobiography, a memoir's focus is on truth, not fact. For example, two or more people can share the exact same experience, and yet come away with radically different memories of that experience. Is one person's memory right and the other wrong? No. The memory of each person is true for him or her. A memoir, then, is a very personal, inherently subjective story recalling incidents that have shaped and impacted one person's life. Even at that, a memoir, again unlike an autobiography, tells the story of a fragment of a life, not the whole of it. *Ordinary Hazards: A Memoir* is a snippet of my story, and it is my story, alone.

It's also important to add that memories rarely come with dates attached, so in some cases, I've simply had to guess the week, month, year, or season a particular event occurred. This, of course, is the downside to waiting until most of the members of your family die before you write your memoir. There are too few people left to consult on these particulars.

Ordinary Hazards was especially challenging as, largely thanks to trauma, I have lost chunks of my childhood memories. There are whole periods of time marked by gaps in memory, and in order to tell my story, I had to figure out a way to bridge them. The notebook entries sprinkled throughout were my way of doing so. The entries also helped me create a sense of sequence. It is often the nature of memoir to jump from one story fragment to another, without attention to strict chronology. But I did my best to create a semblance of chronology here for the benefit of the reader.

The notebook entries were a work combining memory and imagination. Remember, my mother threw away the original notebooks I kept from the earliest years of my writing life. Without the actual notebooks to refer to, I had to use my imagination to construct specific entries filled with the kinds of thoughts and poems my real notebooks included.

During the process of writing this book, I often became frustrated when I was unable to answer some of my editor's most basic questions about the past, so fragmented is my memory. No single person in my narrative, alive or dead, shared my entire journey. I could not even go to my sister to fill in lost memories, as we were separated when I was little more than five years old.

"'I don't remember' is still an answer," my editor told me. "When you don't have a definitive answer to a question, simply say so, and explain the reasons why to the reader," she suggested. This advice was enormously freeing, and I followed it throughout, as needed.

I hope my story helps you to live more fully into your own.

PHOTOGRAPHS

Visual remnants of a childhood,
a meager offering
as photographs go,
but precious nonetheless,
these scattered proofs
that I existed
when few were taking time
to record
the fact
of me.

The beginning of my Ossining years. I would've been five or six years old in this shot. Someone caught me smiling, something I rarely did in those days. I wonder what was on my mind?

With Kendall and baby Brad Buchanan, who I proudly called brothers. I really shot up those first two or three years, didn't I? Kendall provided these precious images. If not for his careful digging, I wouldn't have them. Kendall is still part of my life. Brad passed away long before he should have.

Alone on the streets of Harlem. Maybe this was during one of my visits to see Mom in the city when I was seven or eight. I look lost. A lot of the time, I felt that way, too. I think I came across this after Aunt Edna died, and my sister ended up with an assortment of photos from her estate. I made a copy.

Photo ©: Gary Brewer

Posing in the park at fourteen going on forty! Gail's boyfriend was a budding photographer, building his portfolio. We got a few photos out of the deal! Gary Brewer went on to a career in photography and film.

Photo ©: Gary Brewer

With best friends on the NYC subway, before I chopped off all my straightened hair and went natural. To the left, in her fashionable brim, is Debra Jackson, my friend for life. Gail Broadnax is in the center, the most gifted young writer I'd ever met. I remember being jealous of her enormous talent, and expected her to claim a place in the literary firmament. If only. Gail is gone, now, but Debra held onto this visual record of our threesome. So glad she was able to share it with me for this book.

ACKNOWLEDGMENTS

As with every book, there are people to thank for their various contributions to the making of *Ordinary Hazards*.

Many of the people portrayed in this memoir have long since passed away, so I am especially grateful for the input of the few who have not. Chief among these is my sister, Carol Norwood, who generously made time for my questions and confirmed specifics of some memories.

Thanks to my dear friend Debra Jackson-Whyte who shared key reminiscences that triggered significant memories. Thanks, also, to Debra and my foster brother, Kendall Buchanan, for providing childhood photographs and long-forgotten details. You guys rock!

Thanks to my sister from another mother, Amy Malskeit, for reading an early draft and, more importantly, for helping me grieve the loss of so many childhood memories.

Thanks to my good friend Ed Spicer for your insightful reading of a later draft of this work. Your suggestions were spot-on.

Thanks to my agent and friend, Elizabeth Harding, for boundless support and care of me throughout.

Finally, the lion's share of my gratitude goes to Rebecca Davis, my editor. I cannot imagine having gone on this treacherous and emotional journey without your compassion and gentle guidance. Your meticulous care of this manuscript, down to every word, every metaphor, every comma, contributed mightily to the making of this book. Thank you.